CREATING FICTION FROM EXPERIENCE

Books by PEGGY SIMSON CURRY

FIRE IN THE WATER
SO FAR FROM SPRING
RED WIND OF WYOMING
THE OIL PATCH

CREATING FICTION

FROM EXPERIENCE

Peggy Simson Curry

THE WRITER, INC., *Publishers*
Boston

Library of Congress Catalog Card Number: 64-12149

ISBN: 0-87116-089-7

Printed in the United States of America

To Barbara *and* Michael Curry

CONTENTS

INTRODUCTION

TODAY'S fiction writer lives in a *personal* world, a world closer than yesterday's neighbors. Our thoughts and emotions react to the immediacy of global news, the variety of information and entertainment on our television sets. At times we may fear this world "is too much with us . . ." and endangers our sense of compassion, our sensitivity to the human condition.

Along with this, we witness the continuing changes that affect our profession. We see the rise and fall of magazine kingdoms. We note changes in style and format in the most conservative of popular magazines. We discover great variation in the material and thematic treatment in novels. We find the use of story-telling techniques in long historical and confessional poems, and in literary as well as popular articles.

The fiction writer may ask, "Where is my place in this so personal, so fast-paced and changing universe?" The writer may wonder where to look for his sustaining center, his creative fertility, his energy to generate the written words.

It is a time to remember that the personal, the individual, the intimate view of life has always been the sustaining core of the best writers. The intimacy of the world we live in now serves to provide the fiction writer with a greater need and a wider outlet for his product.

He may trust his sensitive and most personal reactions because they are welcome in the variety of markets.

As a writer and a teacher of writing for many years, I am certain that the greatest need today is the cultivation of our sense of awareness. It is this heightened manner of seeing, feeling, reacting that gives us the material to use in stories suitable for today's markets. A poem by Wallace Stevens, *Thirteen Ways of Looking at a Blackbird,* illustrates the use of awareness in simplified and yet significant form. It may be applied to all sensory re-actions—the texture of water lilies as well as words; the view of faces as well as mountains; the reaction to a dream as well as an everyday chore.

This book, CREATING FICTION FROM EXPERIENCE, deals with awareness as the basic foundation that must support techniques. That foundation has not changed in the changing world, nor will it. The techniques set forth are as relevant as they have always been, and the discerning student of markets will understand how he may vary their use within the range of variation that is acceptable in today's markets.

It is to be hoped that these pages help to awaken in the writer, beginner or professional, an awareness that truly prepares him to discover what he has to offer in our personal world that so demonstrates the great need of man's understanding of his fellow human beings.

Peggy Simson Curry

CREATING FICTION FROM EXPERIENCE

CHAPTER 1

𝕏 Beginning and Becoming

WRITING is a way of life. At best it is a rewarding combination of creative experience and creative expression.
One cannot exist without the other. Memorable writing
can happen only out of memorable living. How much
authenticity and vitality appear in the written words is
directly dependent upon the writer himself. He is the
fountainhead of all his fiction.

This would seem obvious, but it is surprising how
many writers try to start their careers by centering all
their attention and effort on technique. "Tell me how
to plot or characterize," they say. I can only reply that
we must not try to apply methods of expression before
we get to the heart of the matter. That is looking from
the *outside in;* good writing demands looking from the
inside out. Our first—and basic—search as writers becomes the search for something meaningful to say, and
what we must say springs from all that is important
to us.

1

The heart of creative expression

What is *meaningful?* Man, as a creative force, lives not by reason but by emotion. The rich and significant part of the storehouse of memory is filled not with a collection of cold facts but with the multicolored fragments of personal experience rooted in emotion. Emotion is the source of music, literature, of all art. If a man does not feel deeply, he will never create. And all the study of technique cannot pump life into what he has to say. James Stephens has expressed this briefly and beautifully in *The Crock of Gold*: "The head does not hear anything until the heart has listened."

If you have never written a line with the intent of creating fiction, write this one now. It is the best sentence you can write, for the basis of all you may write for the rest of your life is implicit in it. Put it in your notebook. All beginning writers need a notebook, and many professional writers need a notebook. Look at the quotation. Think about it. Relate it to your life by reaching back into memory and taking out those experiences that are unforgettable.

Journey to the written word

Beginning writing is *never* on paper; it is in the mind. It is the recognition of vital experience in our lives. We feel, we know, and we try to put this into patterns. At first we do it awkwardly, painfully. We try to find the right words. We struggle to apply what we have learned to what we do not yet know. It is always a journey from the mind to the written word, and it is always a journey from the known to the unknown. Every short story, every novel is this journey. It is the same difficult and exciting road for the beginner and the professional. The only difference is that the professional has learned to use some technique.

You are starting at the right place if you understand that creative living, unforgettable experience, comes before everything else. What can you do to help yourself along the road toward becoming a professional writer at this initial stage? You can determine to explore thoroughly what has happened to you up to this point in your life. As you search out those most pleasant and painful incidents of the past, your awareness will be stimulated. You will realize that you are beginning to write with a wealth of material. Your reactions to your family, your friends, the world and the people of the world around you have already furnished you with vivid and varied experience. When you learn to recognize and use this material, you will also learn to recognize and use all that happens to you in the future. Once you have become thoroughly aware of the creative potential of the past, you will find yourself more alert to such material as you live each day.

With so much to write about it would seem natural for all beginners to start by putting down strong, believable prose. Such is not the case. Most beginning writers are inhibited. They cannot express themselves because their creative potential is sealed off behind an enormous dam. There are three fears that create this dam and keep writers from trying to say anything worth saying: They are afraid to expose what they really think and feel; they are afraid they do not know how to say it; and they are afraid no one will think it worth saying.

Who can live or write creatively if he is afraid? Let's discuss these three negative ideas that stifle expression. As for the first, there is no reason why you should be afraid to write down anything you think or feel. All first drafts of short stories or books have the breath of life only if they are put down with complete freedom. There is time enough in the light of objectivity, when you are doing revision, to strike out or change what seems irrelevant. And, when you approach publication, there are always excellent editors who can look calmly and critically on what you have done and try to help you.

Remember that the world of writing is a world of unlimited horizons and covers all the variations of human behavior. It is a free country in which you may travel with a sense of pleasure and privilege. In this magnificent realm of the most intimate and the most inspired self-expression, you need not feel a stranger. It is here that all the excellent writers of the past have felt at home and here too you will discover the best writers of our time. This is the world where you belong. Enter it at once by promising yourself to write of all that seems most real and unforgettable to you. Remember that the best or the worst you may put down is not unusual; it is only human. The only passport to the world of writing required of you is your dedication to the expression of truth—the truth of your own experience. And is this not all that is really required of any of us in a lifetime—to express the truth of what we know in the time we have, for the better understanding of ourselves and of other human beings?

How to express what is meaningful

If you are afraid you don't know *how* to express what is significant, be assured that there is much you can learn. Writers never stop learning. No matter how many rules they may know, they discover the great range and variety of word usage only by writing. Today most of our educational centers have become aware of this. Pupils or students can understand what verbs really are only when they discover what verbs can do by way of charging a sentence with meaning—meaning related to their feelings and thoughts. The same may be said of all writing technique: We understand it only as we use it to transfer experience from ourselves to the written page. There never has been and there never will be any substitute for what you may learn by putting words on paper.

It may reassure you to know that some of the most successful authors, Nobel Prize winners among them, have acknowledged their acute sense of inadequacy when starting a new short story or a new novel. They have felt temporary fear that the task before them was impossible, that they could never find the words to say what they wished to say. But it never occurred to them not to *try* to accomplish the task. Fear was put aside by courage, by faith in the ability to complete the job. Every beginning writer who determines to see his first efforts through from start to finish will have established a pattern of work that will help him over many moments when he feels inadequate. Finish what you decide to write regardless of how poorly equipped you consider yourself to accomplish the task. And don't be too harsh with yourself during these first attempts. You are only *beginning*. You are not expected to write with the facility of a Chekhov or a Faulkner. You are required only to write like yourself in the best way you can. Writing is, I repeat, a way of life. You can't expect to accomplish much in the time and space of a few thousand words. You can expect to improve by writing and writing and writing.

Never allow yourself to be afraid no one will consider what you write worth writing. *You* are the person who decides that—not only now, in the beginning, but always. You are the only one who can possibly choose what you should say. Above all else, you must have faith in the worth of what you are trying to put on paper. Every writer must have this faith or he would never write anything. The professional author looks at his own life and at life around him, and one day comes up with the start of a story. He doesn't bother to ask the members of his family, his friends, or the people across the street if this story will be worth writing. He *knows* he is going to write it, for he is impelled to write it— not *compelled* but *impelled,* from the *inside out* and not vice versa. He follows his own inclination or inspiration. He does so because he knows it is this happy and deliberate exploration of his own feelings and thoughts that gives to his work an inimitable flavor and freshness. He knows that lacking this flavor and freshness, the manuscript will be a dud, regardless of how much he knows of characterization, plotting, and the other elements of technique.

No person—not even you—can possibly have any idea as to the worth of your story or book *until after it is written.* It is well to remember that professional writers have learned to accept the possibility of rejection slips attached to what they may consider their best work. When such rejections come, the writers are already busy with new work.

What can a writer learn?

Now, as you are preparing yourself to become a writer, I want to speak honestly of what instruction I may offer. I cannot teach you what you must say. I can only try to help you discover it. I can offer those aspects of technique that I have found most helpful in my own work and in the work of my students. And I must tell you that the best I can say to you may never be enough. I must warn you that to be too conscious of technique can be dangerously inhibiting, that when we become so clever that we always know exactly what we are doing, it is certain we shall defeat ourselves in the initial act of creation. We study and learn in order to become so familiar with technique that we can forget it during the heat of a first draft. Later, in revision, we can look critically at our work and use our knowledge of technique to put the polish on our material. We must always remember that to breathe the essence of life into people on paper is a subtle and elusive act of skill and imagination, of knowledge and reaching beyond knowledge, of the conscious and the subconscious made articulate.

I cannot promise you that in becoming a writer you shall be rich, famous, or happier than you are. I think you will be happier, for every piece of sincere writing, regardless of its limitations, is a small record of the rewarding relationship of creative living and creative expression. I know of no satisfaction greater than that of developing the ability to express oneself fully and accurately.

I can assure you that in becoming a writer you will become a creative reader, experiencing and appreciating as never before the fiction of others. You can never read too much. Reading belongs with writing as country butter belongs with fresh bread.

I cannot promise you will make a living as a writer, but I know you will make a way of life. And somewhere along the way you will come to understand that *the job is everything,* whether you write for small magazines or large ones, for your hometown newspaper, for your friends, for yourself. No writer worth classifying himself as such will be content to do less than his best.

This is a big order. Get started on it now. Look at your one line on the piece of paper. *"The head does not hear anything until the heart has listened."* Begin to explore, through memory, what you have felt, what you can't forget. Pick up your pencil and start putting down words. Be free. You will not be asked to recite in the town square. You are simply expressing what is yours. Don't start fretting about characterization, plot, transition. This is not a finished production: You are simply making a small hole in the dam to release what's there.

Look back, look long, look deep

When I think of becoming a writer, I think of rivers that have no dams. My father gave me rivers. In the beginning there was only one river, but it has cast its influence on all other rivers I have known. This was a small river, is a small river—the North Fork, in the high country of Colorado. It is the source of the North Platte River that flows through the town where I live in Wyoming. There is history along this river, and history in the making. But I like to remember that I know the source, the clear clean spring where it rises, and as it flows from the mountains to the prairies, it carries the melted snows from hills I walked when I was young.

My father gave me rivers. It happened when I was small and hot and tired. We paused at the third bend beyond the ranch house. The sounds of summer were around us—bees and birds, the shuffle of willow leaves, the muttering of water. My father smelled of fish and sweat. He stooped and scooped up the river in his old felt hat and offered me a drink. The hat smelled of dust and sweat and horses. It was stained with machinery grease and two fishing flies were stuck in the band. I drank, and the water was soft and sweet and cool. It trickled down my chin as I drank. Before I finished, the flavor of felt and dust was in the water.

"A man can live without many things," my father said, "but not without water." And then he looked toward the mountains and explained how their snows came down to us and what this meant in terms of grass and cattle and people.

This was a scene that came back to me after my father died. And I thought I could not bear to see that river again. But I went back, and when I stood at the third bend above the ranch house, I wept in the richness of memory that brought back to me a long series of experiences from a magnificent relationship.

Now, at this moment, I can remember love along that river, love and all manner of pain. I can remember death—a fish killing a frog, a dead horse with the dark blue gentians blooming beside him, and cattle drowned and bloated in the high waters of spring. I remember the feel of moss and the designs of it, and the beer-colored doughnut of foam at the bend where I could always catch a trout. By that river I was bitter and angry and lonely, as well as happy and full of excitement. There I confided secret hopes and fears to girls who were friends and to boys who were always more than friends and less than lovers.

Alone in the clover-scented summer evenings I walked by the river and tried to find meaning in such words as "God," "forever," and "eternal." It was easier to be sure about the way the wind felt or the river smelled or how a muskrat sounded hitting the water.

To be a writer is like being a river. It is to carry the life force within you, the green-giving water that rises from the heart, that flows freely with its cargo of images, and in the flowing reflects the shapes and shadows of the world around it.

Where and what are your rivers? Look back, look long, look deep. Discover them again. You will need them always. You will know the first one best, and it will be related to all others in your lifetime.

And yes, from here on we shall talk about technique. We shall try to be clear and practical. But not now. Let the river flow. Without it there is nothing you have to say.

CHAPTER 2

THE ROOTS OF EXPERIENCE

IT IS from truth's high hill that the writer must begin. It is here he must discover what he wishes to say. It is here also where the artist, the musician, the creative person in any walk of life must take his compass readings, must test the wind, and begin his journey. It is a basic place, a necessary place, for all the meanings of existence stem from it.

If the writer does not understand the value of this hill, I do not insinuate that he will never write, or that he will not sell. But I must say that it is unlikely he will write anything memorable. It is doubtful if his short stories or books will have a few of those shining, unforgettable paragraphs that set forth the magnificent reality of heart or mind or spirit. It is not likely that in his writing there will appear those fresh, unique lines that the reader returns to, moved to laughter or tears or filled with the wonder of recognition. The writer cannot give the reader what he doesn't have to offer out of himself.

Awareness and recognition

In the beginning, it is neither technique nor the markets that should concern the writer. It is that he has walked the hill of truth and knows what he must say.

What is this truth the creative person must know? It is all vital experience that strikes us so sharply that a part of us says, "This is real. It is here." It is when the surge of the blood, the clarity of the mind, the twist of the heart tells us life is happening. And, if we are creative people, what happens to us is never enough; we are impelled to capture what we know in the ultimate reality of artistic pattern.

Experiencing truth is what I felt once in the Big Horn Mountains when I looked up from fishing and saw the hills blue with lupine. In that sharp moment of awareness, I thought, "The hawk must think the sky has fallen." Then I knew a poem or a description for a story was in the making; it was happening to me emotionally and mentally.

Truth is what I felt as I was riding in a bus across town and heard the woman in front of me say to her neighbor, "I hate Sunday! *His* mother comes to dinner *every* Sunday." I knew a story was there. Two years later I wrote of an unhappy daughter-in-law and a proud old man in a short story, "Bitter Sunday." After it was published, one of the moving letters I received was from an old man who had written these words in a scrawling, unsteady hand—"The truth in your story has helped me accept the dignity of living alone."

Truth is what I feel when I look into the eyes of a

friend and see the suffering there. Truth is the way the heart moves in compassion toward those who are humiliated, lonely, uncertain. It is also found in situations that provoke laughter or anger. And truth is not always beautiful; it is often ugly, painful, crooked, small. But the writer will find it in its many forms whenever he feels the sharp impact of life.

There are no maps for the discovery of truth. Each writer must find his own way, must learn to recognize the signs along the route. Mountains may leave him cold and the sea inspire him to all manner of dreaming. At the scene of a wedding, for instance, one writer may feel impact because of the music, another because of the way the bride looks at the bridegroom, and another because the scent of flowers gets through to him. The only thing that matters is that the writer feel impact from some source and recognize such impact as vital to his work. It is this process of *recognition* that urges the creative mind to record, in memory or in a notebook, the impression that is there in the experience.

From the moment the writer decides on his vocation, he should know that the hill of truth is around him always. It is there for him to discover. But there are days, even months sometimes, when we exist but are not creatively alive. These are the days when we don't pause, caught up in wonder by the way a leaf shines in the wind's turning. They are the days when the top of the mind is so cluttered that we don't look searchingly into a face, listen to a voice, observe the lift or slump of the shoulders. They are the times when we live a sort of potted-plant existence—neither rain nor sun nor wind can reach us.

The unforgettable click

What can the writer do when living begins to taste like sawdust? He had better make deliberate attempts to climb out of the rut. As long as he stays there he will have nothing to write. He had better realize that to be born with the gift of awareness is not enough; awareness is like a delicate and special plant—it needs extra attention sometimes. He must know that in the life of a writer, the heart must be moved, the mind teased, the imagination nurtured to that sharpness that makes the unforgettable click below the surface of thinking, the click that says somewhere far below what we take for granted, "Hold onto this; let it fasten to you forever."

To find these moments of truth and make them his to use in a thousand different ways, the writer must be willing to try a few simple methods of jarring himself from the rut. He needs time alone, time to let his imagination range widely and freely, time to look at clouds and stars and sunsets. He needs to walk and read and listen to music. He needs to meet new people— people in strange places, on trains, on street corners; a writer cannot afford to stay on one level of the social world. Let him talk freely with millionaires and tramps, with teachers and waitresses, with clerks and artists, with newspapermen and salesmen. Let him seek to understand these people as much as he seeks to understand close friends and family. Let him lose himself in new experiences, for he can never experience enough.

And when he is dull, shut off from that awareness that brings him truth, let him sometimes try a stream-of-consciousness type of writing, allowing anything and everything to flow out of him onto paper. A certain amount of this "freewheeling" clears the air of his world, and soon he will find the gears of his mind meshing into something sharp and meaningful. He will be inclined toward directed creation.

If he feels he knows all there is to know about his own block, his own town, his own family, let him realize that in a lifetime he can't understand too much about his own sky and earth and people and that out of this knowing comes a universal understanding of all men. He must feel that he is always, in human relationships, *moving toward* a universal concept of the meaning of the individual. This is an out-going attitude toward life; it keeps the horizons of the ego from pinching.

There is much to be said for the old idea of "sleeping on a problem." When the writer is willing to do this, he is making a simple and often rewarding use of the subconscious mind. And what the subconscious has to offer is always there; we have only to learn to open the top of the mind so what's below can come to the surface.

The related aspects of the kind of truth the writer must know are fascinating. Once I felt impelled to write a poem about a spring river, a river running that pale amber light one sees in spring and carrying also the frail green that hangs about trees before the leaves are out. It was an image from a river of my childhood where once I had walked all of a cool, earth-and-water scented afternoon (an experience of the truth we have mentioned). I tried to write a poem but it didn't come. Suddenly, in frustration, I threw aside my pencil and paper and got out my water colors. I began to paint feverishly, and I felt the thin cool winds of early spring blowing through the room and I could see that first tenuous green light. My hand gripped hard to the brush, and I had the strange sensation of pouring myself, physically and emotionally, down through my hand, into the brush, and onto the paper. I was painting what I felt about a spring river.

A week later I wrote the poem, and when I read the poem and looked at the painting, I saw at once that they said the same thing. They said, one in color and design and the other in words, that a spring river was love and longing, a delicate promising, a fine high dreaming before the feast of summer when nothing again would be so radiant with the shine of anticipation.

The impact of truth

I have heard music (Debussy for me) say the same thing as the painting and the poem. I know there are dancers who say it with the bending of their bodies. And I also know there are people who haven't seen the dancers or handled the words or held the paintbrush or worked with musical notes, and these people have felt the same impact some early morning or some rain-scented spring night; they have felt it when with friends or completely alone. Truth dwells in many mansions and also in many lonely rooms. And the writer shall know it always by the force of its impact.

In the recording of our moments of experiencing

truth, if we cannot trust to memory, we should jot down a note or two—not too much or too sharply defined, for I have found that too much detail shuts out imagination which should be allowed to come in and add more truth to what is already there. Notes are of no use to me unless the sun can shine through them, the wind circulate freely around them. I recall once writing on an envelope, "March—something annoying about what's left of the snow." I then lost the envelope. Three years later, writing a story, I put down, "Toward the end of winter, when snow pocked the prairie like a nuisance disease . . ." I didn't have to search for these words; they came naturally and easily, for I had recorded that first intruding impression, let it sink below the mind's surface to "ripen," and it came up and out exactly right when I needed it. This is a simple example of why the recognition and recording of our small particles of truth become so vital; they expand into fresh, significant expressions through the combination of memory and imagination.

Creation, the final step for the writer, is like a meaningful religion; it is intensely personal, basically emotional, and in constant process of revelation. And the most fascinating angle of a writer's truth is to be found in revelation. When this is happening, the writer finds himself putting in characters' mouths words that he knows are right without knowing why, discovering in his paragraphs a knowledge he had no idea he possessed. And, wonder of wonders, rising out of the way his words bump up against one another in a sentence is the feeling, the essence of life itself. It is right; it is true; it is alive. We must understand that creation, at its best, is a discovery of the most memorable truth.

There are possibly many explanations for this—psychological, scientific, and fanciful. For myself, I have long accepted the idea that the small fragments of truth gathered in our journey of awareness are the only possible foundation for the linkages of meaning we discover later through memory, imagination, and creation in the symbols of the written word. It is a process so necessary to the writer that he should understand it before he concerns himself with anything else.

Let the beginning writer not ask himself, then, "How shall I write?" or "Who shall publish it?" Let him rather say, "What do I know of truth? What has happened to me and touched me so firmly and finally that I will live with it always?"

And if he can reply, "Once I put my hand on the trunk of a tree and I felt the bark in small, rough furrows under my fingers, and I thought such trees make a house and people will weep and love and laugh under the roof, and the tree is out of the earth and I am somehow related to all of these . . ."—then he knows a little of the span of truth that begins and ends in himself. And he will understand that out of this knowing there will be more than he can say in a lifetime, and much that he will never say as well as he wants to.

CHAPTER 3

ℨ Genesis of a Story

MANY beginning writers feel they cannot write a story unless they have a terrific idea or a cataclysmic event to generate their creative effort. Others expect to bring to a stack of blank paper the complete design for a story, laid out in their minds like a drama unfolding on a motion picture screen. When they do not come up with what they consider an earth-shaking event or idea of a finished story plan, they sit with frozen imagination and dolefully declare they have nothing to write about.

What they do not understand is that *a story becomes, grows into being, in the writing of it.* How can anyone possibly say he has a story until he has written it? What he has, before the story is written, are certain elements that *may* become a story. And in the last analysis it is the words that must speak for themselves—words related in such a way as to bring people alive, evoke thought and feeling, words that create an aura of experience.

The beginning writer should remind himself that few people have the capacity of genius to discover new ideas; that most of the ideas couched in fiction have been with us always and have been used over and over. He should remind himself that cataclysmic events have been here since the world began and in themselves have not the slightest importance: It is how they affect people that makes them significant, and it is only the writer's freshness of approach, his individual slant, that can possibly give meaning to idea or event.

Kindling creative fires

What the writer needs to approach his writing is that genesis or source, that kindling spark that sets his imagination afire. Without this he could spend a lifetime stacking up dead timber in terms of story material and never have anything to start the fire. And fire he must have, for it is creative fire that will provoke and pervade with meaning that important first draft. It is only rewriting that can be done in the cool clear light of objectivity.

The genesis of a story may come from many things, simple or complex—from anything that suddenly sparks the imagination of the writer. Stories have grown from a line of conversation, from a glimpse of a scene, from the sound of a piano, from a thread of emotion, from reading, from memory, from a dream, from family or friends, from being hungry or cold, from falling in love or out of love. Sometimes a major event, such as birth or death, flood or fire, may generate a story, but more often the source is something small, something brief and intense and unforgettable. And by the peculiarity of the creative processes, sometimes the finished story will bear little or no resemblance to the experience that generated it. What the writer must seek, be open to, anticipate and believe in is that first kindling spark; and he can know it only by its effect on him, by the way it stands out, sticks to him, teases him, haunts him, challenges him.

It is always easier to illustrate by tracing one's own experiences, and I will mention here a number of initial sparks that have kindled stories for me. Out of these moments of sharp experience some stories have developed at once. Others have drifted through my mind again and again over a period of years, before anything happened on paper. Some I have not used, and some I may never develop. But I also know that any time—today, tomorrow, or ten years from now—it is possible that one or several of those memorable experiences may start the fire that becomes a story.

The first story that brought me recognition was written when I was sixteen. I was sitting in English class at East Denver High School in Denver, Colorado, and the teacher was urging us to enter the school story contest. The winner would be presented with a book of poetry at the awards assembly in the spring. At that moment I was certain I was never going to become a writer. I was going to die young, for I was too homesick to live. But before I died—there was possibly still time—why not put down what I felt for that cruel and lonely and beautiful mountain country I had left to come to Denver and get an education?

It was a grim and trite story with an equally grim and trite title—"Death at Sundown." My heroine chose suicide on a lonely ridge while her beloved horse witnessed her departure from this sorry earth. She pre-

ferred suicide because disgrace had fallen upon the
family in the guise of a cattle-rustling uncle; she was to
be sent away forever from the country she loved. The
story won the prize, and while the grim and trite
aspects of it do not improve with time, those fresh and
vivid descriptive phrases that conveyed my feeling for
the land and my sorrow at leaving it are as good as any
I could write today.

This story, as is obvious, took its genesis from nostal-
gia, and this in turn produced the elements that
resulted in characters and plot. In the completed work,
the genesis of the story remained as a part of the background and the emotional tone.

My first published story, in a love pulp magazine,
was strong in characterization of two fortunetellers.
The editor stated that it was these minor characters
who sold the love story. What started their creation was
a ranch woman I knew. She had studied fortunetelling
under the instruction of a Hindu in St. Louis and intrigued me by predicting my future with palmistry,
tea leaves, the crystal ball, and the cards. One rainy
afternoon, her hand that was knotted and twisted from
hard work and glittered with huge artificial diamonds,
tapped significantly on the jack of spades. This, she assured me in hushed tones, would be the most important man in my life. And then, for no reason I could
ever understand, I found myself giving her voice, her
gestures, and her words to a large and amiable woman
I knew at once to be Madame Olga. And at that moment there appeared in my mind Madame Olga's husband, a delightful man named Alfonse. I saw him entering their shabby but happy apartment home, and I

heard Madame Olga say to him, gently, "Take off your turban, dear."

In this instance, the story that developed grew from the spark created by a living character rather than from one generated by an emotion.

Unrelated sparks

I now wish to cite three seemingly unrelated sparks that fused to make one story. In June of 1960, I went to California for the first time, and one evening I was invited to the beach for a grunion hunt. Grunions are small sea fish, like trout, and one does not catch them with a hook and line but scoops them up (legally, with the hands) when they are washed onto the sand by the waves. I found this sport most exhilarating, but it wasn't until the reddish-gold moon came up and turned the surf red that I felt the sharp sense of reality that often means the beginning of a story. I looked at the surf and thought, red—the color of life, the color of living, symbol of vitality.

Three weeks later, back in Wyoming, I was asked to talk about writing to an advanced fourth-grade class made up of young people of high intelligence. My experience with the children was fascinating and rewarding, and again I felt that generating spark.

I talked with the children in the morning, and the afternoon of that same day I drove out of town to see an old friend who lives in the prairie country between Casper and Shoshoni, Wyoming. It is a vast and lonely and wind-swept country, not in any way reminiscent of the beaches of California, and yet I found myself thinking of the red surf as we drove across the prairie.

Arriving at my friend's home, I began to tell of the red surf in California and also of my experience that morning with the children. I mentioned that the two situations seemed totally unrelated and yet I wished they could be related. And then it came to me that the spark that might relate them rose from another intense experience. I recalled the death of my father and how cut off from life I had felt, as though a glass curtain had fallen between me and the world. For weeks I had gone around in this strange, isolated state. If the red surf symbolized life, and death meant a glass curtain, could not the two be related as positive and negative aspects of the same story?

Immediately, I saw the episode with the children as a link between the life-and-death situations, for in talking with the children I had called their attention to vital experience with color, sound, and movement. Was it not possible that someone cut off from life might be forced back to it by giving such a talk to children? And it became apparent at once that my main character should be a writer. I thought for a moment of the fact that it is difficult to sell stories about writers and then dismissed this from my mind. I *had* to have a writer to convey my experience with the children. A writer then—a writer on a beach in California, a man not really hearing the surf pound the shore because he was shut away from it by the glass curtain of sorrow. Suppose he had lost his wife and his little girl? Then the episode with the children would be more painful and also more meaningful.

I had my main character then and my setting; I had my climactic episode concerning the children. My conclusion must rest in the grunion hunt and the red moon coming up and turning the surf red, symbolizing life. On that night the hero must break through the glass curtain and back to living. The theme of the story would be that one can bear death only by returning to life.

After I traced the story to this point in my mind, my other two characters were obvious—a little girl who insists the writer talk to her fourth-grade class, and her teacher, a young woman who is part of the hero's awakening.

I tossed these things around in my mind for three days, and then I started for my typewriter. "Night of the Red Surf" was written in half a day, copied and mailed the next day, and sold at once. *Post* editors changed the title to "Heal A Wounded Heart."

Another example of an odd bit of information stimulating a story occurred when a friend visited us on his honeymoon. As he was leaving, bags packed, one hand on the front door knob, he said, "When I get back to Illinois I'll be judging at the horse show." Then he smiled at me and added, "And we'll have roadsters with appointments."

"Just a minute," I wedged myself between him and the front door. "You can't leave now. What are roadsters with appointments?"

Two hours later I reluctantly allowed the honeymooners to go on their way. My husband scolded me for delaying them, and I said, "People can always have a honeymoon—but roadsters with appointments,

that's something!" Five hours later I sat at my typewriter and wrote these opening paragraphs:

> Maybe you've seen King Barton drive at the Kansas
> City Royal, the International in Chicago, or the Western
> Show at Denver. He drove pacers and trotters around all
> the big tracks, but it was in the roadster class that he was
> really famous.
>
> A roadster isn't like a race horse. A roadster doesn't
> compete in races, but he's got to win the judge over in a
> ring showing; he's got to trot with the greatest possible
> amount of action and yet be smooth in doing it; and he's
> standard-bred and must look like a million dollars' worth
> of fancy horseflesh.
>
> King Barton always drove roadsters with appointments
> —the dress-up roadster class. He liked to step to the back
> of his buggy after he'd finished driving, open the buggy
> box, and spread out before the judge his kit of appoint-
> ments: shaving lotion, silver whisky flask, horse brush,
> comb, razor, a bottle of horse liniment and a horseshoe
> —things which might be required of a gentleman making
> an overnight trip in the horse and buggy days. Roadsters
> with appointments carry more prestige than any other
> class, and that's what King liked—prestige.

From those opening paragraphs, the rest of the story
came quickly. I mailed the final copy of "Night of
Champions" to our friend the horse-show judge. He
found no errors in it, and I then sent it to the *Post,*
where it stayed.

Small, brief, unforgettable

A few more brief examples will serve to illustrate
further that stories come from varied sources. A fancy
wristwatch worn by a city dude on a pack trip was the

genesis of a short story of mine published in the *Toronto Star*. A gift of a pair of high-laced boots—a gift I hated—was the spark that began for me, eighteen years later, a story of a girl and her choice between two men who loved her. Three remarkable and stimulating women, all past seventy years of age, provided three sparks for the creation of a fascinating woman in fiction.

All this adds up to the fact that a writer cannot know what may kindle the spark that causes the mind to begin its marvelous and fantastic sorting of the materials that may become a short story. The writer must be alert to anything and everything that might provoke excitement in him. He must seize such bits of unforgettable vital experience and keep them. He should write them down, if only briefly, and he should allow them to move at ease in his mind and let the many-colored lights of imagination play over them. He should believe implicitly that a story can develop from the most trivial experience, if that same experience excites and stimulates him. When he feels the impact of a particular experience, whether it be a fleeting thought, a sensation, something seen or heard or touched or dreamed, he should assume it is a story beginning. And from this assumption he must allow himself the luxury of approaching the material from all angles. He must know that when anything happens to him it indicates that something can happen on paper.

Let the writer explore each brief memorable experience. Let him start writing at once—in his mind. Let him carry the words making articulate his experience; let him take these with him through all his waking hours and also with him when he goes to sleep. If he does so, he will soon have plenty to put on paper. In doing this he knows as much or as little as any writer, for he is in the act of creating a story. Whether or not it will come off, he cannot say, nor can anyone else.

Let the writer be comforted in the knowledge that once his mind works with the initial spark, it is as though a fine wind blew over a small fire, and the blaze that results illuminates much the writer didn't know he possessed—that vast storehouse of material in his memory. In other words, if the writer thinks of it at all, it is impossible for the beginning spark of a story to remain isolated. It is the nature of the thinking process, known and unknown, to add and subtract from everything. And emotion, which is the basis of all creative sparks, does not exist in a void. Emotion is rooted in what the mind relates to it.

A writer wishes to capture completely the initial spark and draw to it all those things that seem meaningful. From the vast knowledge of all he is and has known, the writer has an enormous wealth of material from which he may shape characters, settings, themes, dialogues, descriptions, incidents. Even with all this, the writer will discover new materials he can use as he writes his story, for the way of creativity is the way of adding new dimensions.

If the writer will understand and believe in what is already there for his using, he will not go into frantic mental scurrying for things remote from himself in the building of a story. He will know that what makes the story isn't material he reached out and plucked, like fruit, from a tree standing apart from him. What makes the story is the tree the writer allows to grow from deep in himself, sprouting from that first small seed of impelling interest. It is the tree watered by the writer's blood, fed in the soil of his memory, and towering toward heaven in the sun of his imagination.

CHAPTER 4

❦ THE CLIMATE OF IDENTITY

WHEN any writer, amateur or professional, is impelled
to write what he considers a serious book, it seems to
me he must move into what I can best describe as a climate of identity. A book that says something should do
two things: It should explore the privacy of the writer's
mind and invade the privacy of the reader's mind. To
achieve this dual purpose, the finished book is neces-
sarily a definition of the writer's identity; it is his
psyche translated into objectivity, the personal made
universal. Or, through empathy, it is, in the words of
John Donne, the writer "involved in mankind."

From the moment a writer begins to conceive such a
book until the last revision, he lives in the climate of
identity. He expresses to the best of whatever ability he
may have that which is particularly his, that truth of his
experience. Imagination, that basic tool of art, bridges
the gap between the isolated writer-producer and the
not-so-isolated reader-consumer.

Memorable emotions

How shall the beginning writer know if he is ready to enter this climate most conducive to creating a novel? First, he must have felt something intensely and unforgettably. It began as a small thing, most likely. I think the majority of stories and novels do begin that way. And in that embryonic stage, small as it was, it sank deep in the writer's mind, stuck like a bur, and began to ferment like yeast. It grew larger, drawing to it like a magnet that which it needed. Then, gradually, it became a fever in the writer, struggling to define itself. Phrases became sentences and sentences became paragraphs. Scenes rose vividly in the mind, as though on a movie screen. The writer heard dialogue. And at last he saw words, not only on paper but on a printed page. The writer was "way out." He had wandered into the climate of identity.

First, let us take up the feeling that generates the ideas. Without this initial and memorable emotion the writer will not care enough to communicate what he has to say. And without the fermentation period, when the germ gathers body and force, the writer will not have that inward growth that demands outward expression.

To amuse, to intrigue, to enrich

Finding the best time to start writing is important. Starting too soon, the writer finds himself in shallow water and is in real danger of being grounded. Waiting too long to write may cool his desire to communicate and make his words dull. I once knew an old ranch hand who wouldn't spend his own money for liquor but would drink that bought by anyone else. He used to stand whittling a match in the shade of the barn and remark with satisfaction, "I can take it or leave it alone." If a writer feels that way about a book he wants to write, he is not ready or he has waited too long.

For myself, the time to start writing is when I *know* down to my very bones these things: No one who has ever lived can say what I am going to say in the way that I shall say it. It is for this I was born. It is the reason for my living. It is what I am destined to give, freely and gladly, no matter how long it takes or how much work is involved, for the good of my fellow men—to amuse them, intrigue them, enrich their living. I am indeed blessed to be a writer. The time to begin saying what is mine to say is now, this moment. Ten years from this moment I could do it no better—if there are ten years left. And yesterday it would have been impossible to put one word on paper.

Egotistical? No. It is merely a deep and calm sense of knowing. I savor the moment. Later there will be many moments not so calm—moments of rewriting, sweating, staring blankly into space. But now, in this one and perfect moment, I have only assurance. If I do not have it, I cannot exist in the climate of identity. In that world there is no place for the doubting, the fearful, the ones who accept at face value that damning cliché—"Anybody can take your place." Not mine, he can't. Not when I am writing my book. "All right," I hear someone saying impatiently, "but let's get to the meat of the matter." (We already have.) "How do we get *started?*"

Yes, I know. I asked this once. I asked a kind and wise man when I was thinking of my first novel. He is no longer alive to encourage beginning writers. His name was Struthers Burt. He lived in summer in a beautiful spot, near the magnificent Teton Mountains in Jackson Hole. And to look at the Teton Mountains is to be born again.

"How do I start writing this book?" I asked timidly.

His eyes twinkled. He seemed to look me over very carefully.

"Why," he said, "you just put a clean sheet of paper in your typewriter and begin."

"You mean—"

"I mean there's nothing to shape into anything until you put words down. Time enough to worry about *how* it's put down later."

He was right. Most amateur writers are worrying about how they should put it down; the immediate and great concern is *what* they have to put down. The most saddening thing imaginable is a writer trying to write with nothing to say. If he understands the climate of identity and is not afraid to live there for a while, he will have something to say.

A writer's uniqueness

A few suggestions that have been helpful may be offered to the beginner who is entering or thinking of entering the climate of identity. When you reach a dead end in the writing, and we all do, open your mind. Listen to music, read poetry, walk for miles, go to bed placing the problem clearly in your thinking before going to sleep and assure yourself that in the morning you will have some insight into the problem. This last suggestion is using the subconscious; let it work for you. Believe that the barrier will be lifted. It's the old-fashioned and practical method of sleeping on a problem before solving it.

It helps in writing a book to have a rich occupational background for characters and their problems, particularly one that hasn't been overworked by other novelists. My first novel, *Fire in the Water,* was about the Scottish herring fishermen, and the colorful and varied aspects of this industry gave much substance to my book. In my second novel, *So Far from Spring,* I used the cattle business as the background for my characters and their problems. Among the many fine things in the New York *Times* review was the statement that the novel might be read as a textbook on the cattle industry at the turn of the century. In my third novel, *The Oil Patch,* I used the oil business and an oil camp as background.

Each of these backgrounds was fascinating to me. On a visit to my native Scotland, I spent thirty nights at sea in the boats of herring fishermen. I learned not only the many methods of locating herring, but what the fishermen thought, how they talked, what they ate and wore. Since I was raised on a cattle ranch, it was natural that I should punch cows, help with branding, fix fences, work in haying fields, cook for a gang of men, run a trap line and learn the art of trout fishing. During the war years I was in an oil camp and as a result of this I know how roustabouts talk and what they think about. I understand the range of a pumper's duties and I have watched a gauger run his "thief" tests for marketable oil. I know the problems of the men and of the bosses and I understand the psychological implications that arise from living in a close, regimented environment where social cliques exist and the individual is faced with the necessity of making his own entertainment.

Blending characters and background

These three varied backgrounds and occupations were most important to my books. Why? They were part of my life and part of the climate of identity. They gave rise to the writer's individual and inimitable stamp of reaction that may be placed accurately in the minds of his characters in relation to plot and characterization. The blending of characters and background is most helpful in giving a book not only color but also authenticity.

In getting set to write a book, the writer should also have a definite time conception. This automatically sets up a frame within which events may take place. It makes it easier for the writer to have some idea, however vague, of where climaxes will take place and how much space may be given to them. It helps with the pacing of the novel. When the occupational background material is decided upon, this may help to suggest the time frame. In the herring fishing novel, for instance, a nine-month period necessary to show the various methods of locating herring was all the time I needed to present, solve, and leave unsolved the problems of my various characters. But in the case of the ranch novel I had to have a time span of at least nineteen years, for it took this period for the daughter of my hero to reach the point where she was leaving home for college. Her presence was the foundation stone of the plot, and the plot could not resolve itself until she was on her own. In *The Oil Patch* I needed a sufficient number of years to allow the promotion of men in the oil company set-up and to show, slowly, the effect of oil camp life on the emotional nature of my heroine.

The whole technical problem of the novel—to reveal the development of character and the passage of time —is less difficult when the writer comes up with an interesting and memorable background and a time frame that is satisfactory to his purposes. The time element tends to give the writer a long and comprehensive view of his book as a whole. The right background automatically helps with characterization, providing motivation, conflict, emotional patterns. These two, time and background-occupation, can be guideposts in the climate of identity, keeping the writer from getting lost in his journey of discovery.

CHAPTER 5

THE REALM OF EMOTION

IT IS emotion that colors our existence, often giving great significance to the most ordinary circumstances. We live most fully in those isolated fragments of experience that are made vivid by emotional reactions. In the best of fiction, we find such memorable fragments linked together in a meaningful relationship which is embodied in form. The vital concern of the writer becomes the discovery of the most vital experience he can really know—his own. In order to make this discovery, he must understand and explore the realm of emotion.

When we say to a friend, "That music makes me sad," we realize at once the poverty of such a brief sentence. A world of uncommunicated experience underlies our words. Perhaps as we hear the particular melody, we are swept by memories of driven rain and wind-moved clouds, of evening harbors haunted by the sound of foghorns, of beloved faces long gone, of dreams abandoned. And in the midst of these we may

have an acute and fleeting knowledge of the briefness
and consuming longing that mark man's days on earth.

The common ground

As writers, we recognize the truth and enrichment of
such an experience. It has made us more aware, filled
us with a sense of being sharply alive, mingled the past
and present with a pervading unity of feeling and
thought. Such experience seems too meaningful to let
go. We wish to keep it, to share it, to lift it out of ourselves so that we may see it more clearly and give it the
aspect of permanence. We also know that people who
are not writers have such experiences or wish to
discover them. The common ground, shared by writer
and reader, that extended country in which each may
set his own horizons, is the realm of emotions. What we
feel, we know and believe above all else, and so do our
readers.

How shall we begin, then, to know best and put to
use this world of emotion? We should first explore
memory. What we find there that is rich in emotional
connotations, we should start using. As examples from
my own life, here are three experiences, briefly presented, that I have used in fiction:

1. My father was bringing me home from country
school in a sled drawn by a team of black horses. We
had fourteen miles to go, and it was bitter cold. A bliz-
zard came up. I began to feel sleepy, and my father forced me, from time to time, to get out of the
sled, cling to the back of it, and stumble along through
the snow. When I could walk no longer and lay weep-

ing in the sled, a thin quilt covering me, my father began to beat the horses with a whip, shouting at them to go faster. I was shocked by his cruelty and remembered with added shock his cruelty to me in forcing me to walk behind the sled. When we at last reached a ranch part way home, my legs and arms and face were numb. A tub was filled with snow and my legs thrust into it. I began to weep from pain as the circulation returned. And then I saw that my father was weeping too as he rubbed my hands. I understood then that he had forced me to walk and whipped the horses because he was afraid I would freeze to death before we reached shelter.

2. I had a pet rooster I loved. I found him when he was only a small ball of fluff floating on top of water swirling through our corral after a cloudburst. As he grew he became mean to strangers who entered our yard, charging and pecking at them. My parents said I must give him to the neighbors who would "use" him or let them destroy him. I decided I would kill the rooster, but when I got the axe, he looked at me, making a throaty crow of affection and trust. I couldn't chop his head off. Instead, I allowed my parents to give him to the neighbors who, I knew, would eat him. I hated myself for not having the courage to kill and bury him.

3. When I was in the fifth grade in town school, it was customary to have a large valentine box on Valentine's Day. I had a crush on a boy two grades ahead of me. I didn't have enough money to buy a fancy valentine for him, so I made one. I cut out varying sizes of hearts from red paper and pasted them on a long piece

of red ribbon, the largest heart at one end and the smallest at the other. Then I folded the valentine and put it in the slot of the big hatbox the teacher had decorated and kept on her desk. On Valentine's Day we had assembly, the fifth, sixth and seventh grades gathering for the passing out of valentines. When the teacher took my homemade valentine out of the box, part of it was broken. Some of the hearts had come loose and part of the ribbon, smeared with glue, dangled before the gathered pupils. The name of the boy I had made it for was lost on one of the fallen away hearts. "Whom is this for?" demanded the teacher, a stern old maid. I had to be silent or reveal to the pupils that I was in love with Frederick and had made him a horrible makeshift valentine while other girls had given the boys they admired beautiful store creations. I felt terrible, but at last I stood up and said in a squeaking tone that the valentine was for Frederick. Everybody laughed, and I felt like dying, but Frederick —bless him—with all the ease in the world walked up and claimed the valentine, unperturbed by the hoots and hollers of his contemporaries. He thanked me graciously and kindly. Wherever he is today, I still remember and am grateful.

Even as I recount here these episodes, there come over me the related emotions and related sensory details. I see again my father's contorted face as he shouted at the horses and struck them, and I smell the wet wool and body odor that filled the ranch house as our clothing dried by the fat, round stove. I recall the drift of willow leaves into the low September river as I sat by it weeping because I couldn't kill my rooster. I remember the lips of the teacher, a stubble of hair making a pale shadow above them, as she said, "Whom is this for?" Her hand, forever etched in my mind, was painfully clean and cruelly thin, like a claw squeezing the life from my own heart as she held the mangled chain of paper replicas.

Reality plus imagination

Not only the emotion but also the recollected details in which such emotion is rooted are invaluable to the fiction writer. The vividness of such detail transferred into the lives of characters gives as nothing else the feel of living to the material. And this brings us to the second point the writer must understand and be able to use in his creation of moving fiction. He must learn to transfer his emotions to his characters, letting these created people transfer personal experience to the reader. Our characters become the vital link, connecting our realm of emotion with that of our readers. It is in the act of making this transfer—from writer to characters—that reality becomes art through the use of imagination, and discrimination in the handling of words.

We begin to know what can be done with characters by writing first of the people we know—family, friends, acquaintances—and finally of strangers. In every story or book I have written, there have been the strangers—those people who seem to spring full-blown from nowhere. I am sure I know them very well, although we have met only in the world of imagination or in shadowy corners of the subconscious. I know them because I have looked into myself and into those who are close to me. When I can know my own emotions, I can know theirs, though on first meeting, I do not recognize them at all. The point to be made here is that no man is a stranger in that all encompassing realm of emotion. Fear, hate, love, despair, hope—these do not hide behind the faces of any one color, race or creed.

What I have felt of humiliation, greed, ecstasy may be felt by Cousin Jim when I write of him, adding a little of Uncle Bill as I go along, and perhaps combining these with some characteristics of the man across the street. What I have felt of courage, defiance, tenderness may also be felt by the stranger in my story—the character who comes drifting in, unexpected, stepping through the open door that flies wide in the heat of creation.

We must learn to trust the authenticity of what we feel and to be assured that it is natural and right for our characters to have the same emotions. It is the writer's capacity for feeling, his lust for life, that gives him the foundation for his writing. He expresses such feeling better to understand himself and for those who read for the same reason. In the end he is speaking not only for himself, but for all those who want to but cannot.

Because of the variations of emotional response, we are always discovering in ourselves and in others new facets of behavior. Whenever we are touched, astonished, bewildered by what we or others feel, we may be sure such material belongs in our fiction. *We can create emotional impact through our characters only by acknowledging what makes the impact on us.*

Sensory reactions trigger emotions and are inextricably bound to any memorable incident in our lives. And sensory reactions are also bound to events in the lives of our characters. The reference to music in the beginning of this chapter was triggered by sound which in turn set off memories that dealt with sound, touch, sight, and a trend of thinking. Day by day, if we live with awareness, we have sensory reactions that put down their emotional roots in memory. These are of the most vital importance. Why? Because it is not enough to *say* that a character feels as we have felt or might feel. If we are to reach the reader, really reach him so that he lives in the pages of our material, *experiencing for himself,* we must stimulate his emotions through sensory reactions. We must draw him into the story as though he were the character experiencing the emotion. This is not easy. It is the peak of excellent writing.

Atmosphere and symbolism

And I come now to the discussion of those two related aspects of fiction that are the mark of the artist in the profession of fiction writing—atmosphere and symbolism. It is in atmosphere and symbolism that the emotional realm reaches its culmination, where meaningful communication between writer and reader, via characterization, is most illuminating and unforgettable. Stories distinguished by such communication are those to which the reader may return again and again, rediscovering the well of his richest experience, finding the water of that well fresh and inexhaustible. Every writer who dares dream—and who does not?—hopes before his time of writing is over to offer even a few small paragraphs of such a vital source.

First, let us understand that atmosphere and symbolism are *effects*. If we cannot achieve them in our own work, we can at least recognize and appreciate them in the fiction of others. Atmosphere and symbolism are the *result* of excellent writing technique expressing the most private and meaningful world of the writer. The sensitive reader, in turn, finds in symbolism and atmosphere representations of *his* most private and meaningful world. At best, they offer writer and reader ever-expanding areas of meaning, some of which may be explained and some that cannot be explained.

There is such an intimate relationship between symbolism—which in its richest meaning escapes classification—and atmosphere that it is impossible to consider one without considering the other. For the sake of clarity, we must first distinguish between setting and atmosphere. Setting, as the word indicates, means the locale of a story, the place where characters are in duel with their difficulties. Setting, drawn from the writer's experience first-hand or from his reading or the recounting of others, may be adequately presented in descriptive phrases that give the reader a picture and a knowledge of place. Atmosphere does more than this; atmosphere is *the result of presenting the physical details in such a way as to create emotional reactions.* There is dramatic effect. We have, as a result of emotional implications, a *suggestive aura* produced, and this aura may affect characters as well as readers, may permeate part of a story or all of it.

A writer can create atmosphere only when writing about a setting that has affected him. The most memorable setting, as well as the most memorable characterization, is presented by those who take the trouble to look carefully, to experience deeply, and to express themselves freshly and freely. It is impossible for a writer who feels keenly about any part of the earth to write of it without creating some atmospheric implications. The writer's feeling always determines what he will use in description as well as in characterization, and his capability of saying it is proportionate to his sensitivity to words, his awareness not only of their outward explicit meanings, but also of their overtones of personal connotation. For instance, is the word he wishes to use amber, umber or brown in describing autumn grass in the light of early afternoon? It's possible that under certain emotional reactions he—or the character he is writing about—might see the grass as umber amber brown. If the light is not brilliant, the character might consider it a dull or dead brown. If the sun is thin and bright, there would be amber there. If frost has brought tinges of red into weeds surrounding the grass or mingling with it, a lonely man or woman might see it as an umber fire moving over silent hills.

I wish to make clear here, if I have not already done so, that while we think of atmosphere as an effect related only to place or setting, it may be found inextricably linked to plot and characterization by the very use of effect-producing words. The writer cannot always understand—nor should he bother to try—why one grouping of words may convey only the literal or surface meaning of what he is trying to say, while another grouping of words may move the reader beyond this to several meanings and to the awareness of emotional effects. It is sufficient that the writer know his own feeling as a reality, discover the word combinations that seem to suggest such feeling. It is sufficient that he recognize that aura of suggestion in all excellent fiction—whether it arise from the presentation of place, character, or event—that produces effect. I can define such an aura only as atmosphere.

To return to sensory reactions out of which we create atmosphere, we know them in our memorable incidents of experience. As we recall the pain or pleasure, we recall its accompanying detail. But we must also be open to new sensory experience, to recognize and grasp quickly—before they are gone—those fleeting emotional responses that may become a part of what we have already known, added to an old scene lifted from memory or imagined from a fragment of scene. If we are aware enough to feel it, to catch it as it happens, we have made it ours, and a month or a year later it is memory or a page in our notebook to refresh memory.

Somehow, we must be able to see the world freshly from time to time, discovering new impact in what we take for granted. There are times when I think every writer should become an artist or for a time fill his life with art galleries in order to broaden his association with color. Color, like sound or fragrance or certain experiences of touch, may stir our emotions. Becoming aware of painting through using the brush or studying the work of others impels us to look more closely, to discover astonishing and satisfying aspects of landscapes, people, cities. I have been so struck by the shape and shadow, the whole combination of moving winter grass before a background of blue-white ice-locked river that I have felt exhilarated for days. Out of such experience, the mind soars, set in flight by emotion, and drunk, as though on love and wine, one tosses words in exciting patterns, juggling their meanings to exactness.

Interviewing a naturalist at his home in Jackson Hole one February day, I happened to notice on the porch a piece of old bark on which tree moss was growing. This living green, velvet textured, symbolic of spring, existed on the gray and weathered bark that brought to mind old fences, old houses, things fading against the inevitable encroachment of time and weather. To me the bark and the moss was a life-and-death thing, a hope-and-despair thing, exquisite in its natural combination of textures, colors, and shapes. I asked to bring it home, and I have it yet. How long the green shall be I do not know. Sometimes when I look at it, I make small poems. Sometimes I make men and women who speak from wastes of sorrow in terms of hope. Sometimes I make strange landscapes with green evening skies and gray plains that steal the green in their rivers, robbing heaven. Sometimes I hear muffled folk music. And sometimes there is nothing at all but a most filling sense of satisfaction as I look at it. Yes, I know. It has happened to me, sensually, through my senses. It is the stuff of atmosphere, and I am using it.

There is nothing more effective in the creation of fiction than the use of atmosphere. It helps to produce an artistic whole, a connected meaning of men and events that serves to exemplify theme and produce symbolism. *Atmosphere prepares that intellectual and emotional soil from which symbolism may grow.* It does this because of its suggestive aura that invites imaginative interpretation.

What is symbolism in literature? It is that which has in it a variety of meanings, emotional and intellectual. It is, at best, a splendid extension of human awareness. It differs from allegory in which the specific and *only* meaning is pointed out to the reader. As a student of mine aptly put it, "Allegory lays it on the line." There is no room for private interpretation. There is no need for imagination. Symbolism presents a different world. Imagination opens the door to that world. It allows the reader to bring to a piece of fiction his private universe of imagery. He may follow with interest the surface or literal meaning of the story. But beyond this there will be shades of meaning, implications that allow him to investigate additional intellectual concepts. The most memorable symbolism goes even further; it speaks in the language of the dream that is embodied not so much in scenes as in the essence of those scenes, not so much in words as in the luminescent globes of suggestion that envelop words.

Private reality

It is this private and below-the-surface meaning, so often recognized as an emotional reality but impossible to define to our intellectual satisfaction, this language of the dream, that makes it possible to read a fine story or novel again and again. We return to such a piece of fiction because we have recognized the elements of our dreams which always escape complete definition but which, by their very intangibility and personal significance, we are always attempting to define. In writing, such symbolism comes from the most fertile imagination exploring the mind and attempting to bring up from the subconscious to the conscious level those intangible elements of truth—intellectual and emotional. Since it is the intensity of feeling that often kindles the vivid flash of imagination that illumines a brief intellectual concept of such truths, we are forever seeking further understanding of what we know best only in the realm of emotion.

What man experiences most fully emotionally, knows intuitively but cannot explain away intellectually, is embodied in the world of symbolism. It is not strange that we should desire to express ourselves in symbolism or to recognize ourselves in the symbolism of artists, for the very world in which we live impresses upon us certain unforgettable and unexplainable effects. In the pavements of cities reflecting lights after rain, in spring nights murmurous with wet wind, in the violence of storms, in the nostalgic fragrances of autumn afternoons pervaded with the promise of snow, in old houses touched by the thin shadows of winter trees, in the defiant or supplicating postures of human beings and animals—in these we are moved to discover our own strange longings and dreams. And while we cannot completely understand or express such longings and dreams, we know they define our existence in its most meaningful terms.

Man, at his most rewarding level of existence, cannot relegate himself to a particular niche and pull the world in over him. He cannot exist in a small cave of comfort, living on the stale scraps of old and easily digested experience. He can only move out and stand freely in what light there is, experiencing again, and then exploring what he has experienced in the limitless universe of his own thought and his own emotion.

CHAPTER 6

Of Time and Transition

TIME begins for us the moment we are born; we have
lived an hour, a day, a week, a year. Within each of
these measures of time, things have happened to us,
and we have caused things to happen. Time indicates
movement and change, a river-like going forward that
carries us along. But time is a two-way river: We can
go backward, through memory; we can also keep relating the past to the present and speculating on the
future. We speak, think, and feel in terms of what happened yesterday, what is happening today, and what
may happen tomorrow. In a few moments of the present, we may roam freely over the past. We may move
not only through past events of our own lives and those
of our friends, but also in history. And we may imagine
future time and life on planets unknown to us.

The framework of time

The writer of fiction must learn to deal with four
kinds of time. He has to select a measure of *chronological time*—a day, an hour, a year, twenty years—in

which the events or episodes of his plot will take place.
Within this estimated, isolated, and artificial piece of
time, he will present the opening of his story, the rising
action, the climax and conclusion. He will have to
understand the use of *flashback*—which concerns relating things past to the present. He must cope with
transitions—those time-links or arches from scene to
scene that give the impression of forward movement
of the story. And he will have to become aware of *timing* or *pacing* within the story itself.

Chronological time is the first and easiest problem
of the writer. It is often readily determined by the
nature of his material. The occupations, backgrounds,
problems of his characters will indicate, at least loosely,
the time pattern needed. If the writer knows what he
wants to say, knows his characters, and has some ideas
as to the plot or design for his story, he will have
thought in terms of time before he starts to work with
pencil or typewriter. If he has visualized scenes in
which "this will happen and then that will happen and
then . . . ", he will have some conception of chronological time. When the writer has worked on paper or
in his mind to establish the opening of his story, the
situation set up in that beginning, he should be able
to establish the chronological time necessary to the telling of the story.

In setting up an idea of chronological time, the
writer should not feel restricted, for many stories may
require more or less time than he has allotted. But it *is*
necessary to establish an idea of time, for this very act
forces the writer to look more closely at his material
and the handling of it. He becomes more selective,

working more intently with what he has to say and who shall say it and in what circumstances. Time, in this sense, becomes to the fiction writer what the size of the canvas becomes to the artist: It is a limited and limiting dimension in which experience may be interpreted.

Flashback refers to events of the past that may bring needed information or rich emotional content to the story. A discussion of flashback in relation to the *substance* of the story will be found in the next chapter, "Flashback—The Flavor of Experience." In terms of time, the beginner should feel free to use flashback briefly and casually, as it is used in life. If, for instance, in a scene, the writer doesn't wish to stop the flow of conversation or action by lengthy explanation, he may resort to brief flashback; such as,

a) "He had met her years before on the small beach by his father's summer cabin, when her hair was in pigtails and the same defiance glinted in her eyes."

b) "She recalled that last week her sister had mentioned a neighbor with two small children."

c) "He had ridden a horse once before, when he was eight years old, and he had felt the same sense of impending doom as he did now while he heard the calm voice of Anne saying, 'Take hold of the horn with your left hand and reach for the stirrup with your right.'"

The beginner should remember that long flashbacks clog the action of a fast-paced story, and that some stories—those with emphasis on physical action or struggle—need little or no flashback. If, in his study of short stories, the beginner sees how the author has used the brief flashback to convey information or to build up the present scene by creating suspense, he will begin to understand how it is used most effectively. The obvious problem becomes, *when* to use flashback and *how often*. It is probably a safe rule to say that in any scene of fast action, the less flashback the better. If the reader is gripped by the present, the past only intrudes in the action story.

Technical information from the past should be presented as unobtrusively and quickly as possible. Information that lends insight into the characters or evokes emotional tones should be presented in brief or lengthy form according to the pacing of the scene. If a scene must be slow-moving to convey what the author wants, flashbacks may be longer and more detailed. In such scenes, the author is not so much concerned with the *movement* of the story as with the *depth of characterization*.

The time element troubling many beginning writers is the use of transition. If the writer will remember that the word transition implies *change*—change of place, mood, circumstances, time—he will do better. He will be able to think in the from-here-to-there, from-this-to-that, from-now-to-then sense of writing.

In moving from one paragraph to another and from one scene to another, the simplest and most natural way to approach the problem is in terms of time references—"The next day," "In the morning," "A week later." From such introductory words, the reader is readily moved from one place to another, from one mood to another, from one circumstance to another, from paragraph to paragraph and from scene to scene.

In varying transition scenes, the senses may be used

as posts on which to tack transitions stretching from one part of a story to another. "He *heard* the morning train whistling . . .", "The *fragrance* of lilacs came to him as . . .", "When he *felt* the first *cold touch* of snow . . .", "He *saw* the shadows deepen. . . ."

Emotional reactions may be used as transition posts: "His anger left him as he went out to plough the spring fields and . . ."; "A sense of desolation went with him along the road . . ."; "Fear still shook him the next week when . . ."; "Boredom dominated her days until the telephone rang again and . . ."; "She wept months later when she found. . . ."

References to weather by the author or through the characters may be used in transition paragraphs. Author: "The snows came over the valley, closing roads, obliterating familiar landmarks." Through a character: "He watched the snows come over the valley, closing roads, obliterating familiar landmarks."

A few more suggestions concerning transition devices will help the writer discover additional ones: "The children, going back to school, made him realize summer had gone"; "Christmas decorations began to appear in a few store windows"; "The river was breaking up"; "The ducks had gone from the pond in the pasture"; "The meadowlarks were singing again when he heard from Julie."

If the writer will keep in mind two things about transitions, he will find his task clarified: 1) Transitions cover those parts of a story the writer doesn't choose to put into dramatic scenes; and 2) transitions give the reader time to catch his breath after the intensity of dramatic scenes. This leads us directly to the fourth kind of time the writer must deal with—that of pacing or timing within his story.

Pacing and story rhythm

Each story has a rhythm of its own; it is, by the treatment the author chooses to give it, potentially slow-moving or fast-moving. The more detailed and introspective a story is, the slower the movement will be. Action stories, concerning themselves more with physical activity than with psychological implications, readily assume a faster pace. But in any story the writer's problem is *what* to tell, *when,* and *how much.*

The opening must start a story moving. If the writer has written a page and we are not intrigued by what he has *told* or *shown* (in opening scene) about the main character, then he has failed. The author has not been sufficiently selective in his material to make each line count. It is especially important to do this in openings where the author is *telling about* his character and the situation rather than presenting a scene with dialogue and additional character or characters. Readers are not so readily held by *telling about* as they are by *being thrown into* scene where they participate in action and reaction; they must be *involved* and not made to remain outside the story.

Regardless of the type of opening the writer uses, at the end of the first page he should ask himself what he has done for the reader. Has he clarified character and setting, indicated personal difficulty of his main character or made that character so interesting the reader can't refrain from knowing more? Has each paragraph added to the reader's knowledge of character and situation, or is the story no further ahead at the bottom of the page than it was in the beginning paragraph? Is there confusion of material because the author has tried to tell the reader everything all at once?

Opening paragraphs or pages that *do not* affect the reader or the characters should be taken out. It is a safe rule to follow that if the opening page of a story affects the characters, it will move the reader. Whether this is done through *scene* or through author *telling about* is of little importance. It is "characters in trouble" that intrigue the reader.

When the beginning seems too slow for the rest of the story, cutting and condensing may help.

A difficulty we all have to struggle with in writing is the developing of scenes of mounting interest. If we have a story with three major scenes linked by transitions, we may find the first scene is vital and the other two trail off and become ineffectual. The pacing or timing has gone wrong because we have told too much in the first scene; we have pointed too strongly toward solutions; we have killed suspense. Sometimes such a situation may be remedied by toning down the opening or first major scene and shifting some of the material contained in it to the second and third scenes. We may round out the part we have deleted by additional descriptive material that adds movement, emotional implications, or introduces some new sidelight on the character. If the writer has *good material* to work with —believable and interesting people, a story to tell about them—he can shift material from one scene to another and achieve better timing or pacing.

If a story—or a novel—moves too fast, one may throw in transition paragraphs or a transition chapter to slow it down. In my first novel, the action and development of character went forward at the pace of a fast express until, toward the last of the book, my editor commented, "You know your material so well it's racing like a horse toward the barn door. Is there some way you can slow it down?" Carefully examining the last third of the novel, I came to the conclusion I couldn't make changes within the chapters for fear of destroying what I had achieved. I decided to throw in a chapter that would halt the avalanche, give the reader a chance to recover from the fast action, and somehow improve the novel. I wrote a chapter about an old peddler and his horse coming to the village on a customary trip. The chapter does nothing for the main characters in my story; it sheds no light on their problems. It is merely a chapter that reveals local color and introduces a man and a horse and a business that have no connection with the rest of the book. It is slow, pleasant reading in itself. It serves the purpose of slowing down the pace of the novel. By this contrast, it makes more effective the action chapters that follow.

In the same way, a short story may move much too fast in the scenes, and yet the scenes may be very well done in themselves. When this is the case, the writer may use his imagination and throw in a page or a few paragraphs that will improve the over-all pace. It is like putting on the brake while driving a car down a mountain. Sometimes it's a good idea to take a look at the scenery, be aware of the weather, speculate on things in general; one can't do this and be driving fast.

Time is a control device in the hands of the writer. In understanding the *chronological* time of his story, the author narrows his range and sharpens his focus. In understanding *flashback,* he adds information and depth to his characterization. Working with *transition* and *timing,* he regulates the speed of his unfolding journey in experience and relates the parts of that journey in the most convincing and interesting manner.

CHAPTER 7

⚑ FLASHBACK—THE FLAVOR OF EXPERIENCE

Too frequently writers assume that the technique of flashback refers only to factual information which is presented in order to clarify present situations for our readers. It is true that this is one function, the most limited function, of the flashback. In this narrow use of technique, we merely acquaint our reader with fact in a casual manner. We *report* for the reader that which has gone before the opening pages of our story or book. When I write, "She had learned to fish years before on her uncle's ranch in Colorado," I am using a factual flashback to clarify a present scene in which my heroine is going fishing. I am *reporting*, and I am *plugging* a situation by giving needed *information*. We use this simple form of flashback in those scenes where we do not wish to intensify the situation or impede the forward movement of our story.

But there is a second and most significant use of flashback. The writer should understand that flashback forms the emotional foundation for what he has to say; he must create the *flavor* of experience by this excellent device. It is flashback, used in this manner, that makes passages of writing stand out, intriguing the reader to return again and again to the words, finding in them special and personal meanings, experiencing deeper emotions.

To begin to understand this use of flashback, we must accept a definition: Flashback is that which has happened before. When something "has happened" to us, what is involved is emotion, not factual information. Memory, in life as in fiction, is that basic ingredient which gives color and meaning to our existence. It has been said that what we do not remember has never happened. This is true for the writer, for his fictional characters, and for his readers. What we *do* remember —or choose to remember—provides those things upon which imagination may work most effectively.

New wholes from old parts

Let us at once clarify our conception of imagination. I like to think that imagination is making new wholes from old parts; it is creating new meanings from old experience. Memory is the storehouse of the *old parts* from which we fashion our *new wholes*. It is by this method that we reach beyond the personal to the universal, finding the new meaning expressed in art forms.

Let us look more closely at our "old parts." It is as natural as breathing to recall aspects of our past experience. But we recall most sharply that which touched us in the past when the present deeply affects us; depth of immediate feeling is always supplemented and intensified by what has happened before. Living is never a series of isolated emotional experiences, but, in its essence, is an overlapping of experiences. The first hill we remember sheds its impact on all other hills we know. The first love of a man or woman is bound to be all later loves. Comparison is inevitable when man reflects upon experience.

As writers, we cannot be too much aware of the mnemonic aspects of all creative work. In the fictional world, such aspects are monumental. What people have felt most intensely must, if they are creative people, become the foundation of what they have to say, of the imprisoned reality of the printed word. Such material, that rich and inexhaustible storehouse, is tucked securely in memory.

Flashback, in its most effective use, is the recollection at the right time in the present of that which has been most meaningful in the past. When the sharp moment comes, when we are triggered into emotion, back we go in memory to relate to the past. It follows that at this point we may ask ourselves, Where do flashbacks come into best use in fiction? From our experience, the answer is obvious: Flashback is most significant in fiction as in life—in those scenes that deal with deep emotion. When we write of love, sorrow, joy, bitterness, disappointment, fortitude, it is natural to move out of the immediate scene to a sense of the past. We may, in such fictional circumstances, link the present and past with striking effects.

Technically speaking, this linking of emotional scene to emotional scene, from present-to-past and back-again-to-present, may be done in two ways. We may use *similar* scenes or *contrasting* scenes. In my novel, *The Oil Patch,* there is what I consider an effective death scene in the oil camp. It is true that this scene could have stood alone and been satisfactory. I wanted it to be more than satisfactory; I wanted it to be memorable. To help achieve this, I added a flash-back scene in the mind of the character dominating the stage at this time, a scene in which he recalled his first experience with death when he was a boy in grade school. I believe that each scene was highlighted, com-plemented, made more meaningful by the other, al-though they were of *similar* nature. Both dealt with death.

In the following quotation from the immediate death scene, the reader will note that a line of transi-tion carries him smoothly from the present to the past:

> Shorty raised his pale and haggard face. "Max boy, don't leave me."
> Max sat down beside him. "I'm not going anywhere, Shorty." And he stared into the blue evening that moved across the monotonous rows of brown houses, and all the rooftops shimmered as though they rose under water, and he heard the wind whimper as it came in from the prairie and prowled around the buildings. And while he waited in the long minutes before the coming of the women, his mind went back to his own first experience with death and from yesterday a part of his youth stood out in clarity and sharpness. . . .

After this transition, I left a space and went into the beginning details of the flashback, working slowly to-ward the climax of this scene from the past:

> He looked fearfully and at the same time curiously at Violet's face and he was filled with wonder. He had seen death on the animals at the ranch and it had been stink-ing and ugly, but Violet looked like a big sleeping doll.

He thought she was very beautiful. And it wasn't until he saw the red barrette in her brown hair that he started to cry.

Our main character had, of course, bought the barrette for the girl, but he had not been able to give it to her before her death. At his mother's suggestion, he had sent it to the family of the dead girl, and they in turn had sent word that "Violet was wearing it and he could come to see her if he wished." We swing from the flashback to the immediate scene with another line of transition:

> Now, in the brown house on Poverty Row of Crow Camp, the scene faded from his mind as the door opened and the women came in quietly and moved about the room, speaking softly, their handkerchiefs touching their eyes. Their skirts rustled and their heels tapped gently on the worn floor. Max took hold of Shorty Blackwell's calloused brown hand and pressed it hard, as though in that mute gesture he spoke of Violet Arnold and Alice Blackwell, and of himself caught in the shadow of sorrow that linked him to the gray-headed roustabout.

You will notice that both scenes, past and present, are blended in the last line of the above paragraph, giving an over-all sense of unity. It is well to do this when possible where past and present scenes are used within a chapter of a book or within a unit of a short story.

The effective use of contrast

Contrasting scenes are equally striking in bringing about enriched emotional tones through flashback. In my first novel, *Fire in the Water*, I used this method.

The immediate scene was one in which my hero was swimming in the sea, recalling with sorrow and a sense of futility the death of his father who had drowned at the harbor mouth. Had I used *similarity* of flashback, I would have allowed my hero to recall a scene of death in the fishing village or at sea. Instead I chose *contrast*, the hero's memory of swimming in the same place, climbing onto the same rock to rest in the sun on a beautiful day when he felt there was only joy and good in the world, when he was enchanted with living. This use of contrast served to deepen the tone of sorrow in the immediate scene.

These two examples of the technical use of flashback point out how added richness of emotional tone, producing in turn added richness of meaning, may be created in a short story or a novel.

If we stop to consider what this added richness may mean to our readers, we immediately see that it rounds out the tone of our work, for it provides a common emotional ground where author and reader meet. Our readers are constantly using memory; they think in flashback whenever they encounter emotion, and sometimes produce emotion by such thinking. They recognize the *truth* of such flashback situations in fiction and accept our characters as people of flesh and feeling. They live vicariously in our characters, and through the implications set up by their own experiences, *go beyond the pages of the book or story*. It is this act of projection beyond the written word that makes for enriched and memorable reading. It is an evocative experience for the reader. Under such circumstances, a reader may say that an author has described in great detail a room or a landscape or a character when the author had done no such thing. The author has drawn the reader along the hypnotic path of emotion, left him alone, and then the reader has created his own minute details—drawn, you may be certain, from the reader's memory.

When emotional foundations are certain and solid in fiction, we may truly say that a good story or book begins long before the opening paragraph and continues beyond the final paragraph. How do we explain this elusive but most meaningful aspect of fiction? For other readers and writers, I cannot speak. For myself, I am certain it is inextricably bound to memory and is achieved in the creation of fiction through the technique of using similar and contrasting flashbacks.

What your characters remember

We may say, then, that the flashback thoughtfully used gives us rounded rather than flat characters in our fiction, creates empathy in our readers, enriches through the use of imagination not only the writer's world of experience but also that of his readers. By this single technique, understood and practiced, we may avoid monotony, surface characterization, thin emotional tone, and shallow fiction that says nothing. It is my personal conviction that it is impossible to achieve any depth of characterization without looking into the memory of our characters. And surely it is impossible to write without looking into our own. Until we examine the old parts, there is no horizon of new wholes.

Flashback is part of our daily living. Who among us has not walked through autumn hills and recalled similar scenes of dying splendor, similar feelings of the transitory nature of things? We have also recalled on such walks the living green of spring. We have been acutely aware of those somber aspects of existence that seem to rise unbidden to the foreground of the mind—nostalgic, sad, harmonizing with time and place.

Perhaps in concluding our discussion of the flashback, that vital aspect of all creative work, it is sufficient to say that each day of our living is followed by the wide wake of memory which, at a given time, may rush forward to inundate the present and cast its peculiar influence on the future. This is the cumulative nature of being. Out of it comes the best we have to say for ourselves and for our readers.

CHAPTER 8

✗ VIEWPOINT—A PERSUASIVE LIGHT

THE materials of a story may be compared to a landscape enveloped in darkness until the writer discovers
a point of view he considers most suited to his material. Then it is as though a powerful beam of light
came on, illuminating certain high peaks of action and
emotion, shadowing particular valleys of story movement, suggesting distant plateaus of character development. Guided by the light, the writer starts his characters on their inevitable journey via the written word.

Viewpoint involves a special relationship between
the writer and his material. At best, it is a condition of
complete rapport; it is that persuasive light in which
things outside and inside the story characters become
most believable to the writer and, he hopes, to the
reader. And although all story material may be presented in many lights, from many points of observation, there is always one particular viewpoint or
combination of viewpoints by which the writer's material reaches the most effective expression.

Trying out viewpoint

The beginning writer will not feel so frustrated in dealing with viewpoint if he will remember that he has been working with it since the beginning—since he thought of writing a story. He has, whether he realizes it or not, been considering viewpoint relative to all parts of his material—the setting, the plot, the characters, the theme or substance of what he has to say. This is because the writer cannot think in terms of story material without trying out viewpoint.

The writer may say to himself, "Jim Jones opened the door and saw the empty house"; or, "I opened the door and saw the empty house"; or, "I was with Jim Jones when he opened the door and went into the empty house and stared at the dust on the floor." The writer may also say to himself, "The house had been empty for a long time and it was a surprise to the town when Jim Jones returned to it. He had never been a man of sentimentality and had refused to discuss the trouble with his wife, who was a woman of great charm." This is trying out viewpoint to see how it feels and fits. It is using a part of the story material in search for a persuasive light in which to present all parts of the story material. It is a *way of looking*, a method of focusing the light where we think it may work best.

In trying to find a way to best tell the story of Jim Jones, the writer has presented the material through the eyes of Jim Jones, through the eyes of a friend telling about Jim Jones, and through the omniscient or multiple viewpoint in which the author comments on the house, Jim Jones, and his wife. The writer has tried

out the three basic points of view used in fiction—
1) *major character,* 2) *minor character,* and 3) the *om-niscient.*

Considering these three basic viewpoints, the writer
may realize that while Jim Jones is the major character,
the story may not come off best told through major-
character viewpoint: "Jim Jones opened the door and
saw the empty house." He may also discover that he
feels more at ease writing from minor-character viewpoint: "I was with Jim Jones when he opened the door
and saw the empty house." It is possible that the writer
may decide to use the omniscient viewpoint: "The
house had been empty for a long time and it was a surprise to the town when Jim Jones returned. He had
never been a man of sentimentality and had refused
to discuss the trouble with his wife who was a woman
of great charm."

Each of these viewpoints has advantages and disad-
vantages in relation to the author and his material. The
story could be handled in any one of them. The viewpoint selected by the author is dependent upon his understanding of his material and his ability to handle
the viewpoint he considers best. Sometimes a writer
cannot really understand his material until he is in the
act of writing it or has finished writing it. There are
writers who can work well in major-character viewpoint
but turn cold when they attempt minor-character viewpoint. Some writers are able to handle the omniscient
viewpoint from the beginning of their careers and
other writers can never handle it.

In attempting to understand his material as he
searches for viewpoint, the writer should first ask him-

self, what is this story about? The very substance or
theme of some stories will determine the viewpoint,
for the meaning of any story is directly linked to the
author's feeling, his sensing of the story's potential.
The writer should also ask, whose story is it? In trying
to answer this question it is often easy to determine
whether there is one major character or two or more
characters who may be classified as major. The writer
may also be helped toward finding a suitable viewpoint
by asking which of these people feels most sharply the
conflict in the story. He should try to decide which one
person he, the writer, cares most about. Who is the
one person in the story he thinks he knows better than
the others? Who is the person he can feel most at ease
in presenting through scene and narration, through
identifying with and through *telling about?*

The "eye-witness" narrator

In starting to write, most beginning writers feel at
home in *minor-character viewpoint*. Almost all stories
done in minor-character viewpoint are handled in *first
person*. So rare are those stories in which minor-character viewpoint is presented in third person that for
practical purposes we'll confine our discussion to the use
of the first person.

My first slick sales were stories written in *minor-
character-first-person viewpoint*, which I consider one
of the easiest to handle. In such a presentation, the "I"
telling the story is not troubled by feeling self-conscious, for he is not the main character telling the story
but is telling the story *about* the main character or
characters. He is *reporting* the happenings of the story

as he sees them or as he knows them to be. He is a *bystander*. His role is that of *observer* rather than *participant*. He does not at any time *identify* with any character, moving into that character's mind and emotions. He is a *witness* to the story's development.

Such a viewpoint allows the writer to be objective and yet to present his material with authenticity and intimacy. He is convincing the reader that this happened because he, the "I", saw it happen, knew the people.

Always remember that in *minor viewpoint* the teller of the tale is in a *minor* role. He is never in a *major* role. If he does take a major role—acting or reacting in a significant position in the story development— then we are not in *minor-character viewpoint*.

Bystander-telling in first person works well in presenting any kind of story material and is ideal for the reminiscent, nostalgic type. The beginning writer, who must learn first to use his own memories before he can become aware of going beyond them, will find himself comfortable in minor-character viewpoint.

As an example of minor-character viewpoint with reminiscent flavor, I quote the opening paragraphs of a short story of mine, "Osage Girl," first printed in *The Saturday Evening Post:*

> When I remember my Uncle Jed, I always see him the way he looked that day in Springfield, sitting easy on the sulky behind Osage Girl as she paced a half length ahead of the field of nine. That was the greatest race I ever saw my Uncle Jed drive.
> My Uncle Jed was a big man. He was over six feet tall and he weighed two hundred and ten pounds, but he walked lightly. There was nothing clumsy about Uncle

Jed. He had a round red face and hair that was white even when he was young. . . .

Sometimes in using the minor-character viewpoint it is easier for the writer to present his material through "we" rather than through "I." In such stories, the opening scenes and the bulk of the story are written through "we," and the author occasionally moves into the "I" for a particular scene. In stories where I have found the "we" more suitable, there have been not one but two or three characters occupying a dominant position in the development of the story. As the reader may gather, in the story just quoted Uncle Jed is *the* leading character, and it is *his* actions and reactions that make the story.

Examples of writing in which the "we" was more effective and in which I switched occasionally to the "I" are taken from "The Secret of Bogie Bill," another *Saturday Evening Post* story.

Opening paragraph using "we":

> We drifted into the valley late in July. Gabby came from Iowa, the drunken Swede from cutting timber in Washington, and Bogie Bill from dealing in Reno. It was the third summer we'd worked for the boss and he said we were the best hay shakers in Colorado.

Paragraph in the middle of the story with a switch to the use of "I":

> The gun went off then, just as the Swede moved, and I saw the surprise on his face and how his mouth came open. He fell loose and quiet, like a sheet blowing down in the wind. Gabby turned and came running back. He fell on his knees beside the Swede . . . The little guy came up and put handcuffs on Gabby, but Gabby didn't

seem to notice. I heard the little guy tell the boss how much money Gabby had stolen. The boss had a strange look on his face. I guess it was as hard for him as it was for me to believe that Gabby had stuck up a bank . . .

Bystander or participant

Major-character viewpoint is widely used and may be done in first person or in third person. Since we have just finished discussing the use of *minor-character-viewpoint-in-first-person,* we'll take up the use of *major-character-viewpoint-in-first-person.* Telling a story from this angle the writer is always more than *bystander;* he is a *participant* in the story. He identifies with one *major character,* usually—but not always—with *the* dominant character in the story in the role of hero, heroine, or villain. An outstanding story in this viewpoint—distinguished by its unity, coherence, dramatic suspense and psychological implications—is Poe's "The Cask of Amontillado":

> The thousand injuries of Fortunato I had borne as best I could; but when he ventured upon insult, I vowed revenge. You, who so well know the nature of my soul, will not suppose, however, I gave utterance to the threat. *At length* I would be avenged; this was a point definitely settled—but the very definiteness with which it was resolved precluded the idea of risk. I must not only punish, but punish with impunity. . . .

Presenting a story in first person through the major character is the "confession" method of writing, in which the protagonist reveals intimate aspects of his own life. Stories told in this viewpoint are found not only in the confession magazines but also in magazines ranging from those of large circulation to the literary and experimental publications. In these stories, as in those done from minor-character viewpoint, we have a great sense of authenticity and intimacy. We also have the same restrictions—we can know what the teller can present only through *his* knowledge of the situation.

Some writers cannot handle this kind of first-person writing because they feel self-conscious; it is difficult for them as the writing "I" to speak freely of their courage, wit, or reactions in making love. Love stories done in this viewpoint, however, are very popular, if the author has the light, humorous touch such as that characteristic of Willard Temple's stories in the slick magazines. Frank O'Connor uses the first person most effectively in his witty stories presented through the major character.

Deliberate limitations

The writer has more freedom using the *third person through the major character.* Here the author may identify with the "he" or "she" in the story and may also enrich his characterization, settings, and incidents of plot by commenting on one or all of them. In some instances in the *major-character-third-person viewpoint,* the writer stays within the confines of his character. He decides to present *all* material *through* this character. He does not supplement his identification with this main character by commenting on another character, on the scenery, or on some aspect of the theme or plot. This is the *third-person-limited* approach. The author *restricts* himself because he feels more identity with the protagonist this way or because

he doesn't care to attempt to deepen the story by adding the supplementary material. The writer must be
guided by his own instincts in his decision. The average
beginner will understand viewpoint better if he will
try to confine his first work in *major-character-third-
person* to the *limited* approach. Here is an opening paragraph from a short story of mine, "The Lady Loved A
Jailbird," published in *The Saturday Evening Post*.
The viewpoint is major-character-third-person and is
third-person-limited:

> Judith stared through the kitchen window of the farm-
> house, her long hands idle in the dishwater. She could see
> the stretch of field, green in the green evening, the brown
> patch of plowed earth next to it, and, farther on, the
> shapes of the Wind River Mountains. A sweet-sad aching
> began in her heart. *I am so big*, she thought, *and so plain*.
> Only when Tommy was here I felt different; Tommy
> *made me feel the magic*.

As this story develops, I never leave Judith's viewpoint to give an objective panoramic description of the
land, to make a comment on Tommy, or to otherwise
allow myself to step out of Judith. I completely identify
with her, deliberately holding the viewpoint within the
limits of her eyes, her thoughts, her emotions.

I have indicated earlier that many stories in major-
character-third-person diverge into *author comment*.
This does not mean that we change viewpoint; the
viewpoint of the story is still that of the *one major character*. The first example of this that I would like to
mention and quote from is James Joyce's story, "The
Dead." The major character in this story is Gabriel,
and as the story moves along, it is given over more and

more to his viewpoint. As it reaches the climactic pages, we are immersed in Gabriel's thoughts and emotions. But, in the opening paragraph of the story, the author comments on Lily, the caretaker's daughter, who is employed as a maid:

> Lily, the caretaker's daughter, was literally run off her feet. Hardly had she brought one gentleman into the little pantry behind the office on the ground floor and helped him off with his overcoat than the wheezy hall-door bell clanged again and she had to scamper along the bare hallway to let in another guest. It was well for her she had not to attend to the ladies also. . . .

Joyce goes on to comment on other characters in the story, moves into Gabriel's viewpoint, comments on other characters as the story progresses, but returns again and again to give the bulk of the story over to Gabriel. In these concluding paragraphs, we find indication of how completely we have been put into Gabriel's viewpoint.

> The air of the room chilled his shoulders. He stretched himself cautiously along under the sheets and lay down beside his wife. One by one, they were all becoming shades. Better pass boldly into that other world, in the full glory of some passion, than fade and wither dismally with age. He thought of how she who lay beside him had locked in her heart for so many years that image of her lover's eyes when he had told her he did not wish to live.
> Generous tears filled Gabriel's eyes. He had never felt like that toward any woman, but he knew that such a feeling must be love. The tears gathered more thickly in his eyes and in the partial darkness he imagined he saw the form of a young man standing under a dripping tree. . . .
> A few light taps upon the pane made him turn to the

window. It had begun to snow again. He watched sleepily the flakes, silver and dark, falling obliquely against the lamplight. . . .

As an example of a *major-character-third-person* viewpoint in which I comment on part of the story material related to plot and background, here is an opening paragraph from "The Bride Wore Spurs," published in *The American Magazine.*

If you're up in the valley you might still find a Big Lee saddle hanging in one of the barns. There are a few left but folks won't part with them, for Big Lee's become a legend. Of course, saddles have changed, and now all the cowpokes ride the ones with bull-moose trees that became popular along with rodeos, but old-timers will tell you that no one can make a saddle the way Big Lee did, shaping it exactly right for a man and putting it together with good leather that would stand up to all kinds of wear and weather.

I go on to comment on Big Lee and the conditions prevalent in the valley at the time of the story; I mention incidents related to the plot of the story. Six paragraphs later, I move into the viewpoint of my major character, Big Lee:

Big Lee took a piece of leather out of the soaking tank and put it on a marble slab on his work table. He found a big darning needle and began drawing the head of a Texas longhorn steer on the wet leather, and let on like he didn't hear the ranting of the men.

As the story develops, I stay strictly within the confines of Big Lee's viewpoint. At the conclusion of the story, however, I revert to author comment:

Folks in the valley will tell you that Big Lee killed ten men that morning, but Sara knows the truth. Sara's ninety-two years old and you'll find her at the home place on the North Fork.

I conclude the story as though I, the author, were interviewing Sara. The story is entirely done in third person—the major portion of it through the eyes of the major character, Big Lee—but the story is properly introduced and concluded through *author comment.* There was no other way I could give my readers the knowledge they needed before the story proper began and after the action was completed. Such a divergence in viewpoint, occurring at the beginning and the ending of a story for the purpose of introducing and rounding out the story's meaning is known as a *frame.* Frames are always presented in author comment. And author comment is always in the *omniscient* point of view, but this does not mean that the dominant viewpoint is the omniscient. We are speaking here of *major-character viewpoint* in the third person. In using this, as can be readily seen, we have two choices: We may use the *limited,* the restricted method in which we never diverge from identification with the major character, or we may *supplement our identification* with the major character by adding *author comment.*

All-seeing, all-knowing

Skilled novelists prefer the *omniscient* viewpoint because of the varied textures and wide range of novel material. Many distinguished short story writers of the past and the present also prefer this view. In using this method of presenting his material, the author establishes himself as all-seeing and all-knowing. He maintains a detached and impersonal point of view.

In this position, he can comment freely on any or all of the characters in his story. He can focus the light on vast panoramas of information, moving from past to present or vice versa. He can also focus directly, at any time, on one particular character, moving in for a close-up. He can go into the minds of two or more of the characters, completely identifying with them. The complexity of life is best presented in the omniscient point of view. It is not a viewpoint that is easily mastered by the beginning writer. He should understand and be able to use freely *minor-character viewpoint* and *major-character viewpoint* before he attempts to use the *omniscient*. There are so many variations in the use of the omniscient point of view that it requires a skilled hand and a perceptive mind to create an impressive whole from story material.

An example of one use of the omniscient—that in which the author treats all the characters impersonally and grants them equal importance but does not identify with any of them—is "The Ambitious Guest" by Hawthorne. Notice how clearly here in the beginning he establishes that detached and impersonal viewpoint he is to maintain throughout the story:

One September night a family had gathered round their hearth and piled it high with driftwood of mountain streams, the dry cones of pines, and the splintered ruin of great trees that came crashing down the precipice. Up the chimney roared the fire and brightened the room with its broad blaze. The faces of the father and mother had a sober gladness; the children laughed; the eldest daughter was the image of Happiness at seventeen; and the aged grandmother, who sat knitting in the warmest place, was the image of Happiness grown old. . . .

Stephen Crane used the omniscient viewpoint in his story "The Open Boat," which begins with these lines: "None of them knew the color of the sky." As the story develops, he treats each of the four men in the boat with equal emphasis. However, Crane moves closer to his characters than Hawthorne, for he does not remain detached at all times. He turns the spotlight on each man in the boat and supplements this with specific and panoramic descriptions of sky and sea. There are four major characters in the open boat. We see through their eyes and also through the eyes of the author.

Hawthorne's use of the omniscient viewpoint is entirely detached and objective, while Crane's use of the omniscient point of view is a combination of detachment and identification.

In considering the three basic viewpoints—*major character, minor character,* and *omniscient*—the beginning writer should remind himself that the best stories of the past and the present have been written in each of these. He should also recognize that excellent stories have been written in first as well as in third person.

Occasionally stories mix third- and first-person viewpoints. The writer will find this in some of the works of John Steinbeck, J. D. Salinger, John Updike and other authors. He may come across this *mixed viewpoint* in some of the small literary or experimental magazines. It is much harder to put a story across in this way than by the use of one of the accepted and proven methods of presentation. The beginning writer may wish to try experimental work, but he had better wait until he can

handle the conventional and more marketable viewpoints.

Outside influences on story viewpoint

Even though the beginning writer may understand
the three basic viewpoints and understand the use of
first and third person relative to these, he may find himself in difficulty. After trying out viewpoints, finding
one that fits and in which he feels at ease, and one that
logically seems right for his story, the writer may not
be able to put together a story that comes off. This happens because the writer cannot foresee the result of
viewpoint in the actual *writing* of the story. In this
creative process, other factors enter in: dimensions
change as the writer puts his story together and he must
recognize the necessary element of looseness.

No viewpoint is set in concrete, although writers
sometimes mistakenly think so. We hope to come up
with the right viewpoint before we start writing our
story, but we can never be sure. It is only when
the story has run its course in the heat of that first draft
that we can begin to see it as a unit and to consider the
sum of its meaning.

We must understand that as writers our choice of
viewpoint is inextricably bound not only to the whole
experience of putting together the elements of the
story, but also to extraneous influences that are remote
from the material and the writing of the story. I have
had the texture of weather—not related to any scene in
my story but present on the day the *idea* for the story
came to me—intrude on my handling of the material.

Sometimes I have had to shove aside forcibly such intruding imagery, and at other times I have had to
change the climate of an entire story to suit this peculiar influence. And in this seemingly minor change, I
had to make a dozen other changes. I would like
to mention a few viewpoint changes necessary because
of influences outside of the story material itself, in order
to make clear what I mean and in order to offer insight
into similar circumstances that may arise in your writing.

The first story I sold to a major market was based on
a character sketch of a man I had never met and a sport
I had never witnessed at the time of writing the story.
My husband had an uncle who was well-known as a
driver of pacers and trotters. As my husband told me
about this man, I wrote a character sketch, in first person, talking of him as though he were *my* uncle. I then
gathered from my husband all the information he knew
about harness racing, the "lingo" of the track, etc. Soon
I had the incidents that promised a story. I thought the
story out in *third-person-major-character, through* the
uncle and *about* him, using *identification* and *author
comment.* When I started to write, it didn't work; I
had dead material on my hands. I went back to *minor-
character viewpoint,* first-person bystander telling the
story as though he were *my* uncle, and all went well. I
am sure that the *circumstances of acquiring this material* influenced the viewpoint. There was no logical reason why the story shouldn't have come alive in major
character, in third person, but I lost all feeling for it
when I tried to write it that way.

In a western story not designed for popular readership, I had to change viewpoints after I had the story underway. The story contained what I believed to be a scene of justifiable adultery. When I tried the story in third person, major character, I was astounded to find the climactic scene, in which the major character did commit adultery, offended my sense of good taste. I rewrote the story, and it still bothered me. I then switched to bystander point of view, in which the outcome of such a scene was subtly planted and hinted. The story came off with fine tone and unity when related by the minor character in first person. There was no question of taste in my conception of the material. It was a thing that entered into the story after it had been written. I am certain I could never have published this story had I insisted on presenting it in third-person-major-character viewpoint.

Recently I came up with characters and incidents and an idea that promised a salable story. I sat down and wrote freely and happily, confident that everything was just right. A few hours after the completion of the story, I read it over and was shocked to find it dull. I again considered my characters, the incidents, the basic idea, and was still convinced the right ingredients were there. What had happened?

In the beginning, I had thought of writing this story from the viewpoint of the character I liked and knew best. Previous to my going to the typewriter, however, a young woman similar to the heroine of the story had stopped by to see me, and I had felt an overwhelming sympathy for her situation. After her visit, I started to write the story from the girl's point of view, although originally I had intended doing it from the man's point of view. My greatest *sympathy* in this case was with the heroine, but the character I *liked best* and *felt most at ease with* was the man. It should have been possible to tell this story successfully from either viewpoint, but it hadn't worked out that way for me.

I threw the old copy on the table, went back to my typewriter, and using the same material, the same opening situation, I did the story quickly from the man's point of view. It came off with fine sparkle and pace and sold at once. I think this would have happened the first time had I not been interrupted by a caller whose plight aroused my sympathy to a high pitch.

When the writer, then, considers the possible viewpoints, chooses one he thinks right, and yet finds the story doesn't come off, he should shift to another viewpoint. Also, he should examine his initial feelings about the story and decide whose shoes he, the writer, wears most comfortably. He should ask himself if some outside influence, some unexpected turn of events, has crept in to distort his original decision on viewpoint.

Often writers ask about the desirability of switching viewpoints in the middle of a story, of transferring the "he" third person from one character to another, of turning from John's story to make it Mary's story. To this I can only say that it is better not to do this unless the story material demands it for greater meaning or greater clarity. In all instances, such a switch should be avoided *unless the story becomes stronger by making the switch*. For every story in which viewpoint switches, there are thousands accepted in which the viewpoint remains the same throughout. It takes great skill to switch viewpoints within the established treatment of a story—and get away with it.

Beginning writers become confused in reading or writing *third-person-major-character* stories in which passages appear that are not directly identified with the major character. They think there has been a change in viewpoint. "I am not seeing through Mary's eyes," they say. "Here is a whole half page in which the author talks *about* the weather, the house, the characters." What they are concerned about is *author comment* used to supplement *major-character viewpoint*. This, as I explained earlier, is a brief use of the omniscient, but is not *the viewpoint* of the story which is tied to Mary, since the greater part of the material is presented through her actions and reactions.

Exercises that pay off

The related elements of viewpoint may be greatly clarified by the study of printed stories presented in minor character, major character, and the omniscient viewpoint. The writer should recognize that in *minor-character viewpoint,* the author—as bystander—tells *about* the characters; that in *major-character viewpoint,* the author *identifies* with *one* major character, telling the story *through* this character (limited) or telling the story *through* this character *plus author comment;* that in the *omniscient viewpoint,* the author may treat *two or more characters* with equal emphasis, may comment freely whenever he wishes, and may even *identify with two or more characters.*

It will be helpful to the beginning writer to practice changes in viewpoint by doing a story in *minor-charac-*

ter-first-person and then switching to *major-character-first-person*. If he will follow this by presenting the same story in *major-character-third-person* (limited) and in *major-character-third-person plus author comment* and in the *omniscient,* he will have helped himself to understand what viewpoint may achieve in a story. This is a trying and tedious exercise, but it pays off in the facility with which the writer, following this experiment, is able to use the appropriate viewpoint in all his writing.

In examining the material of experienced writers, the student of writing will discover that some stories are handled very *objectively*. Everything about the characters is indicated by their actions but never *told* by the author. In other stories, the author not only states aspects of characterization by commenting, but also goes inside the minds of the characters and writes in a stream-of-consciousness manner. In such instances, the author is writing from the *inside of the characters out* and not using *surface* indications through emotion, gesture, manner of speech, etc. This is *subjective* handling of story material. Many fine stories are combinations of objective and subjective treatment of the material.

As an example of a combination of objective and subjective writing, here are two paragraphs from a novel of mine. The first paragraph is *objective,* and the second *subjective.*

The rider had pulled up his old black horse and sat slackly in his saddle. He was a small man with wisps of white hair sticking out from under a dirty black cap. . . .

She tried to be calm, tried to think of peace and sleep and God, but instead she felt terror and anger and a need to defend her identity. She was fighting as though the end of the world had come, but she made no sound. There was only the perspiring horrible struggle. . . .

The second paragraph is the *inside* anguish of a woman suffering in childbirth.

The beginning writer should be confident that he *can* understand the uses of viewpoint. He can recognize that he is trying out viewpoint from the moment he starts to consider his material in terms of story. He can accept the fact that sometimes the right viewpoint will come to him readily and that at other times he will not be sure until the "rightness" is evident in the actual writing of the story.

If the result, the completed story—which is more than the sum of its parts or the author's conception of it—stands strong and meaningful, the writer knows that his viewpoint has been successful. How he discovered this viewpoint—through trial and error, through insight, through accident—does not matter.

CHAPTER 9

✕ THE TOUGH AND TENDER PEOPLE

THE best of the self must be given away in the act of creating a good short story. This is the outward push of the inward fire. To whom shall we give our moments of awareness, our intuitive understanding of human relationships, our ideas that are never new but must appear so in the morning freshness of our imaginations? We must give them to people who are as real and human as ourselves.

Love—or curiosity

What does this mean to the beginning fiction writer? It means he shall be dedicated to a search for characters, for people who can portray his personal world in universal terms. And he should ask himself at once, before he enters the long and difficult years of writing, if he really loves his fellow men or if he is merely curious about them. Under the clinical observations prompted by curiosity alone, human beings may be reduced to the level of rats in a laboratory. Without warmth of heart, the writer cannot practice empathy, that identi-

Brushoff," it is the events within the margins of the printed pages that determine that my tough kid will not always be so, that his life will be straightened out from this point on.

A third practice I indulge in is the mental portrait painting of people I know. I apply this only to people who intrigue me. To do this, ask yourself what it is about a certain man or woman that stimulates, disturbs, or baffles you. Ask yourself why you remember one individual and forget another. Try to eliminate all the things you think of in the confusion of putting down the first impressions, and settle for the one dominant aspect of the man or woman or child that stands out—or that you are able to make stand out after much thought. Try to express this one outstanding or elusive quality in a sentence in your mind. This practice, which I think should be followed whenever the opportunity presents itself, tends to eliminate the trite and ordinary and bring out the sharpness of characters. It also brings to the foreground of a writer's thinking the thing that may excite him into the creating of a story.

As an example of this practice, I must mention again my *Post* short story, "The Brushoff." One night, while idly drinking coffee and thinking how machinery instead of horses had taken over the haying fields, I recalled a summer when I had raked hay on the ranch. I could remember only one of the men on the crew that year, and he stood out sharply. I asked myself why, what was there about him that persisted in my memory? I remembered that I had disliked him, but I had also respected him. Why? And then I realized that it was his painstaking devotion to his work, his rendering of the ultimate of service as a hired man. This was the dominant color of his portrait, the bright strong color of hard labor he had done with pride, forgetting the time, intent only on the perfection of the job.

He was an old man and to use the greatest character contrast, I knew a young man would have to be placed in opposition to him. This gave rise to my tough kid. And to get his character, I reached back into impressions of character gained from meeting and observing boys in a state institution for delinquents. From several sharp pictures of these boys, I formed another that was new and yet had its basis in the boys I had met. I recalled that while I was visiting the institution, one of the teachers told me some of the boys didn't even receive a card at Christmas. I immediately heard my tough kid relating this to another character, saying it with longing and with bitterness, and I knew him to be lonely and frustrated and in need of love. I also knew him to be as belligerent and withdrawn as I would have been under the same circumstances. And what could my old man, dedicated to a life of labor, teach him? At this point, I began to range back and forth over their lives, narrowing down to the time and scenes and setting that would present my story. My characters became, before I put a word on paper, two tough and tender people—a sharp-spoken old man who believed in work for work's sake, for the best job possible regardless of hours or pay, and a boy who had been in reform school and had a chip on his shoulder toward the world, yet wanted desperately the consideration and love he had missed. From this point on, the story rolled out in rough draft.

Reader reaction

In the last analysis, the test of how well we have brought people to life may be determined by the reaction of other people. The editor's check reassures us we have put living characters on our pages. Sometimes there are other things that illustrate this point. In connection with "The Brushoff," there was an unforgettable experience. I had been asked to present a program at our mountain camp for the blind. The director asked if I would read them a story, for many had not yet mastered Braille. I decided I could only read them a story that seemed to me to be warm and human and real. I got the carbon copy of "The Brushoff" from my files and drove to the top of the mountain.

In the bare-floored, drafty, recreation cabin with its dusty smell, I stood before the blind people. My heart went out to them, for I wanted desperately to let them know I cared about them, wanted them to accept me and what I had to say. I trembled, feeling inadequate to the situation, and I began to read about my old man and the tough kid and the haying fields in the summer sun. And as I read, the faces lifted toward me, and the unseeing eyes seemed to search beyond the wall of darkness. It was very quiet in the big cabin with its wooden benches, curtainless windows, and the heap of red embers on the hearth of the fireplace.

When I had finished reading, an old man got up and came to stand beside me. He was very brown-skinned and handsome, and I had been told he was eighty years of age. He began to talk of the haying fields he had known, of the men with whom he had shared bunkhouses and haylofts, and of horses he had driven.

"Your story brought it all back," he said. "I knew fellows like the ones in your story. They were just that way. All you say is so true." And then he spoke with love the names of a few men he had known and the names of his horses. The light lay on his face and his face was beautiful with mixed emotions of a lifetime. It seemed all the warmth of the room centered on him, for the others turned toward him and leaned forward as though they rested and were comforted in the shade of his experience.

I was moved to tears. I could only stand, speechless, and cling to the strong, old hand that touched mine. This is the thing I shall remember long after the money for the story is spent. This was the ultimate reward my tough and tender people brought me.

CHAPTER 10

𝒳 PLOT—A PATTERN CREATED BY PEOPLE

WHEN we consider the four major ingredients of a good short story—plot, characters, setting, and theme—it is plot that looms like a nemesis before most writers. For many years the very word "plot" caused me to break out in a cold sweat. Somehow I had the idea that plot was a cast-iron device, molded before the writer started to write a line on paper; that characters were jammed into it, made to fit and to perform within a rigid framework and that by some magic unknown to man, the writer must create a sense of life and the living within this miserable restriction.

People and their problems

When I could stand it no longer, I simply eliminated the word "plot" from my vocabulary. I turned my thinking toward bringing people alive through their actions and reactions; through my narrated estimates of them; through my identification with them; and through my understanding that if I wrote a story, things had to happen to people, and when things happened to them, there must be problems to solve or leave unsolved. *Plot then became no more than people seeking to solve their problems.* And any pattern set up as to rising action, climax, and conclusion could not be designed by standing on the *outside looking in* but by getting *inside the people and trying to look out.* I had to know the people first, and plot would follow.

Another way of saying this is that all plots are no more than *a history of personal difficulty.* Whether people overcome their problems or are overcome by those problems, the plot of the story is what the people do and what they are—physically, emotionally, spiritually. The best stories—not all, but the best—include the element of *change.* From the beginning to the conclusion of a story, some change takes place—in circumstances, in the characters, or in both circumstances and characters. A good story goes somewhere; it reaches a destination that may be pleasant or unpleasant, good or bad, comic or tragic, or simply satisfying. If another definition of plot is required, it can be said that *people plus plot equal change.*

When we read a story, we may ask if a progression takes place from scene to scene or through a panoramic account presented by the author or through the use of both panoramic account and scene. Panorama is only another word for wide-view narration by the author, rather than the use of scene in which the characters act out the movement of the story, using dialogue, gesture, emotional reaction. We may also ask if in this progression or movement there have been moments of crisis, moments when the character seemed defeated, moments when there was an indication of his licking the problem, moments of pause before the final climax and conclusion. This is a study to ask ourselves *if plot is happening*. It is an attempt to determine whether the main character or characters deal with their problems from a stated beginning to an ending that has *change* implicit in it.

Elements of the plot

It is helpful for the writer to realize at once that some elements of plot may be established *before the writing* of a story, but others can only show themselves *in the process of the writing*. Both aspects of the plot —those conceived before the author begins to write and those *discovered* in the writing—are dominated by character. Plot, like the entire substance and meaning of a story, is something that happens from the moment the writer starts to think about the story until the last revision is completed. It is well to know also that the story is always more than the sum of its parts—more than characters, the plot, the setting, the theme. It exists uniquely in itself, with new meaning, just as a piece of music is always more than the written score, the composer's dream, or the conductor's interpretation of it. And the story, like the piece of music, will have varying degrees of meaning to those who experience it in reading as the listener experiences the music.

By recognizing that there is a *necessary looseness* to plot because of its dependency on character, the writer can overcome much of his fear of it. He can also find reassurance in the knowledge that he has really started the process of plotting from the moment he thinks of writing anything, for in fiction ideas do not exist in iso-

lation but must be tied to people. When any idea is tied
to a person, the writer is at work on characterization.
In conjunction with this, he must think in terms
of time and place and events, of scenes and the space
between scenes that must be filled with transitions. He
is also thinking in terms of *movement*. He conceives
lines of dialogue, bits of description, pieces of panoramic detail that must cover the ground, must move
the reader forward in his knowledge of character-set-
ting-plot-theme. In all of this the writer is plotting, and
he is working *through* or *around* his characters; he is
letting them think, feel, and say some things *for themselves through scene,* and he is thinking, feeling and
saying other things *about them through narration or
panorama.* The craftsmanship of a superior short story
is directly dependent upon how well the author can
handle scene and narration in relation to what he has
to tell.

In superior plotting, background and characters and
actions fit together so closely and blend so smoothly
that it becomes impossible to separate one from the
others. We must remind ourselves that plotting, like all
the aspects of the short story, is interwoven with the author's recognition and realization of his material. He
must be aware of what touches him and then begin to
ask himself what he can do with it. I can best explain
this—which is the process of plotting—by example. I
have selected a short short story because of its brevity
and simple story line which is easy to follow and explain. A good short story has all the elements of
a longer story: It is a story the author has found can be

told in a minimum of words and which, when told in this tight form, is satisfactory to him.

This story, like all short stories I have written, is impossible for me to talk about now without my remembering sharply and clearly the elements from which it grew—how those elements were put together through character into plot, which was the movement toward solution of the problem of the main character.

The first element of the source of this story happened when I was riding down a country road with an old rancher. We turned a corner, and a porcupine was lumbering across the road in front of us. Porcupines destroy timber. They also make trouble for animals; when the nose or any other part of an animal touches a porcupine, the porcupine quills are released. Needle-sharp, they go deep in the flesh, causing pain and infection.

The old rancher stopped his truck, reached for the .22 rifle back of the seat, and stepped out. The porcupine paused, looking up at him with small, dark, bright eyes. The rancher squinted down the barrel, taking his sight, then he lowered the gun and said, "Shucks, I can't shoot him, lookin' at me so alive and trusting."

I had to smile. He looked like a tough, hard-thinking old man, but I knew he was soft underneath. We drove on and came to a small ranch with a deserted ranch house. He asked me to come into the house and look it over. I found out that it belonged to him, but he had never lived there. The empty cupboards stood open; there were no curtains on the windows; no furniture, but thick silvery dust covered the floor. "Fixed it up for my daughter," he said, "but they wanted to live in town—she married a city man."

We left the empty house and drove up on the high range where there were cattle in the highest pastures and sheep in the lower ones. The sheep, their tails turned to the brilliant sunset, were drifting slowly toward lower country and the bed ground. The old rancher stopped the truck, looked at his sheep, and said, "Sheep always go east with the evening. Don't want to look into that bright sunset. Hurts their eyes."

Twenty-four hours later I had the setting, plot, and characters (with the exception of two who came on as a surprise to me) for a short story. The stimulating first incident was the scene with the porcupine; it made me fond of the old man and revealed an unexpected facet of his character. But I didn't really get excited until I heard the line about the sheep—poetic, beautiful. I sensed that the line about sheep had many implications. I considered it as a line in a poem, as the title of a story, as a suggestion for a theme of some sort. The moment I got home I began to think about the old man and the porcupine and the sheep. Certainly there was no story in these three things—not yet. And then I suddenly remembered the empty house from which his daughter had gone. Suppose he had fixed it up because he didn't want her to leave? Suppose he had been determined always to keep the daughter with him and his wife? *Why* had he wanted to keep her?

This is plotting. It is a process that grew out of my being intrigued by the old rancher's behavior concerning the porcupine and by my delight in the poetic line,

"Sheep go east with the evening." I made a definite step forward in plotting when I began to consider the house and ask why the rancher might wish to keep his daughter with him. It was then that I began to see the problem or source of conflict.

A few hours later, after much drinking of coffee, staring out of the window, and tossing ideas around in my mind, I got to the reason for the rancher's problem: The rancher, like the sheep, would not face the fierce light of sunset—the sunset of his own life. He was afraid of old age and death and particularly afraid of facing them alone. This is the motivation for the problem, the desire to keep his daughter with him always.

Now, I have made real progress: I know not only my main character's problem but also the reason behind that problem. My character has been looking east —away from the sunset—as the evening of his life draws closer. And a theme has suggested itself. When a theme grows inevitably out of the author's conception of his material, it gives substance and meaning to the entire story and is the greatest of help in plotting. One knows at this point that one has more than events, more than character, more than setting. One has a strong central core to hold the work together and a core that is part of the main character in all its implications.

Clue to conflict

Nothing has been written on paper at this point, of course. And here it is appropriate to say that the more the author can understand of his story before he writes, the easier it will be to get through that all-important first draft that contains the fierce imaginative fire.

Obviously, the old rancher is to be my main charac-ter. From the beginning I have been thinking in terms of *his* problem, *his* life. I have already been character-izing him, drawing my material first-hand, from life, in his reaction to the porcupine. He, in his own words, has given me the clue to conflict—he had fixed up a house for his daughter, and she had chosen to move to town with the "city man" she'd married. This material surely contains the meat of a workable fiction plot, and I am fortunate in discovering three seemingly isolated things during one trip to the country and being able to find connections that make them related and meaning-ful. But this is only part of the answer. Fiction does not report life but interprets it; imagination must take over fact and add new dimensions. I do not know at this point what the new dimensions may be.

I begin to do more plotting. How shall I present the material I now have? Is there good reason for my pre-senting this material through the rancher? There is, because I feel most sympathetic toward him and be-cause I know him better than the other two characters I am considering for the story—his wife and his daugh-ter. I decide to eliminate the city husband as an "on stage" character; any information concerning him will be given through the other characters. Through view-point, I am beginning to focus on the material now. I am trimming the edges. I know that I have three char-acters, a problem for the main character, and an idea of theme. And, at last, I am ready to think in terms of *writing* the story.

Mental tryouts

At this point, I begin to try out opening lines and paragraphs in my mind. Another writer might try them with pencil or paper or at the typewriter. But for me the opening of any story must be written out in the mind! I hear the words as well as see them. In this mental exercise of writing in my head, I have decisions to make. What format is my story going to take? Shall I plunge at once into a fully developed scene or shall I have a few opening lines of background, a brief springboard to catapult the reader into the scene? Or shall I open with wide-view author comment in a panoramic approach? In asking myself these questions, I keep trying out opening lines in my mind. I am searching for those particular words, those particular lines in which I feel completely at home and in which I also feel a sense of great excitement. Shall I do most of the story *telling about* (panoramic, or limited view) or shall I do most of the story *through* the main character? After trying many lines and considering many approaches, I keep coming back to the rancher and how I feel about him. At last I am sure the best way to present the story is *through his eyes and his emotions*. I have now concluded another major step in plotting—the definite establishing of viewpoint.

Where am I going to fit in the theme? Heaven only knows. But I am sure it will be there, somewhere. I turn my complete attention to an opening paragraph, presented through my main character. I identify with him. This is empathy. I decide that the porcupine scene, taken from life, is as good a scene as any for an opening. It is not a fully developed dramatic scene but merely a brief action scene to serve the purpose of opening the story, establishing setting and character, and hinting at the problem. I go to my typewriter and write:

> Jim Jamison didn't see the porcupine until he'd almost run over it. He slammed on the brakes and got out, carrying the .22 rifle. It was a young porcupine, and as he drew a bead, it turned and looked at him.
>
> "Why are you cryin' at me?" he asked impatiently. "I've got trouble enough now." But he lowered the rifle, for the look in the little eyes reminded him of the hopelessness in Mary's eyes when he'd told her about Sue-Ellen. "Get on with you, Spike," he said, and turned back to the truck.

I must confess that I had no idea at all what the man's daughter or wife would be named until I was writing this opening at the typewriter. In the mental drafts they were merely wife and daughter—shadowy, unclear. I was thinking too strongly about naming and presenting my rancher. At this point in the actual writing, I saw that the wife could be based on a friend of mine whose name is Mary and who would reflect the warm, sincere type of ranch woman who could be Jim's wife. Sue-Ellen was still a question mark. I tell this to help the beginner understand that if he clearly knows and understands his main character, secondary characters often have a way of coming quickly alive in the process of actually writing the story. This situation refers to what I mentioned earlier as "a necessary looseness" in plot. *Don't try to figure out everything before you write. Discovery* is a number one ingredient in plotting and in writing a story.

Preparing the reader

Now to return to the writing. So far so good. By transition, I must get the rancher to the place where his daughter is and create the major scene in which conflict is established. But in order to have this scene meaningful, I must *prepare the reader* by giving information, by covering the ground (panorama presented through my comment as author or through flashback in the mind of the main character). Again, this is a continuation of plotting; it is a choice not only of what information is to be presented but of *how* it shall be presented. I decide to use flashback—past information that will make the present significant to the reader. Again, I am presenting the material *through* my main character:

> He drove on down the dirt road. In a few minutes the buildings of the lower ranch came into view, the red roofs bright in the amber sun, the big barren cottonwood trees towering above them. It was here he had brought Mary as his bride so many years ago, and it was here their daughter, Sue-Ellen, had come only six months ago with the shiny new wedding ring on her finger.
>
> He and Mary had never had either the money or the time to fix up the ranch house for themselves. They'd talked about it a lot, pretending they had money to spend, and they'd planned every room in detail. But the years had gone by, and the house had stayed the same.
>
> Then Sue-Ellen wrote that she and Roy, her husband, would be coming back to stay, and Jim and Mary had moved up to the old house, the original homestead on the

property, which was too far gone to permit any day-dreaming about it. Jim had hardly noticed the moving; all the available hours had been spent getting the lower ranch ready for the day Sue-Ellen and her husband would move in. He'd felt a great sense of pleasure and accomplishment when that day finally came; his and Mary's dream had finally come true—for their daughter.

He got out of the car now and walked slowly toward the house, remembering sharply the money he had spent on it. He'd had it remodeled and had put in a gas stove and electric lights. He'd even started a lawn.

All this is pouring it on in order to make the scene more effective. It is building sympathy for the main character.

His daughter was in the kitchen, packing the last of her cooking utensils. "Sue-Ellen—," he began and then paused, not knowing how to go on. Instead of a young woman of twenty he seemed to see the grave face of a little girl with dark pigtails. For a moment he wished with all his heart and soul to return to that time.

"I'm sorry, Pa," she said. There was a stiff set to her lips, and she did not look at him.

She was prettier than Mary, he thought. Mary had been a sturdy little bride with strong capable hands and a way of walking that set the dishes jiggling in the kitchen cupboard. But Sue-Ellen was like a willow growing along the ditchbank in spring, tall and slender and beautiful.

Jim looked down at his big hands and his heavy wrists. How had he fathered a wonder like Sue-Ellen? And then the pain of losing her came up in him and he blurted out: "Your mother and I—the hard years with nothin' fancy—and then fixin' all this up for you and—."

Note that physical descriptions of Sue-Ellen, Mary, and Jim are worked into this part of the scene and that

more sympathy is built up for the rancher by revealing
the depths of his feeling for his daughter. Also, the
problem, the source of conflict is indicated in the
phrase, ". . . the pain of losing her." We would not be
as sympathetic toward the rancher at this point in the
story if we had not been prepared by *what has come before* this scene. This is an important part of the working out of plot: knowing *when* and *how* to present certain aspects of the material. In terms of *when,* we refer
to this as *timing* or *pacing.* The effect of parts of a plot
is inextricably bound to the element of *timing.* The
pace, movement of the plot, is governed by *when* things
happen through scene or narration or both.

> "I know," she said softly. "But Roy doesn't like the
> ranch. And I—I get lonesome for town, Pa."
> "And so you're pullin' out and leavin' me to run this
> place and the homestead too." He couldn't keep the bit-
> terness from his voice.
> "The boys," Sue-Ellen said. "They'll help you."
> "A fat chance of that," Jim said sourly. "They get
> home from that high school in town and what do they
> do? Mike has to practice the violin. All Joey wants to do
> is ride the calves." He glanced around, seeing the open,
> empty cupboards. "You're not leavin' this afternoon?"

I had no idea until I was writing this paragraph that
Jim would have two sons or that their names would be
Mike and Joey or that one would practice the violin,
another ride the calves. But, as soon as I wrote
this into the story, I could see that it would add depth
and color in a later scene I found myself visualizing
while I was writing the immediate paragraph. This,
the reader should understand, is another example of

what I mean by "necessary looseness" of plot. It is what comes to the writer and fits in as he is in the act of writing his story.

> There was a long silence. "Yes," Sue-Ellen said finally. "Roy's gone to borrow his father's truck. I've got to finish the packing." Then she began to cry. "Don't try to keep us, Pa," she said. "Just leave us alone. We only want to live where we like—."
>
> "And where's that?" Jim shouted. "What's he got to offer you? Where's he gonna work?"
>
> "In a filling station."
>
> "A filling station!" he muttered. He yanked his dust-stained hat lower on his forehead and walked blindly out of the house.

This is the climax and ending of the first major scene of the story. It has been led up to and supported by the opening paragraphs, developed from a low key to a high pitch through the characters, and ended abruptly. Developing scene to the fullest extent is a skill necessary to the execution of plot. Scene reveals characters in *immediate action and reaction*. It is a method of *showing* the reader rather than *telling* him.

Scene props

In deciding which portions of his plot to present in scene and which to present in narration, the writer should remember that *dramatic crisis*, always based on *conflict*, is the ideal material of the scene. He should also remember that the scene needs props, just as the stage scene becomes more effective through lighting, gesture, and set. The author sets his props through in-

troductory paragraphs that acquaint the reader with
the main character, hint of impending difficulty, give
background information that will point up the scene,
and establish setting.

> Outside, he stood looking at the land. He'd paid for
> every acre in sweat and backbreaking labor. And Mary—
> Mary had worked just as hard. For what? For a daughter
> who didn't care about the land or the sheep and cattle
> that grazed on it.
> He drove home, remembering how afraid he'd been
> that he couldn't keep Sue-Ellen here; that was why he'd
> spent so much money fixing up the house, while he and
> Mary went on doing without. The old homestead looked
> shabby in the afternoon light; the log walls were bleached
> silvery gray by time and weather. When he stopped out-
> side the kitchen door, he heard young Mike's violin. Like
> a yowling she-cat, he thought.

This is a transition accomplished through the mind
of the main character. The aspects of the main problem
are given more light in that we know the rancher has
always feared losing his daughter and that this fear mo-
tivated his putting so much time and money in the fix-
ing up of the ranch house for her. And here we pick up
one of the unexpected (from my point of view) sons
who entered the story earlier.

> He walked across the porch and into the kitchen.
> "Mary?" he called. "Where are you?"
> Mary was in the front room. She sat with her hands
> folded, a soft smile on her face as she watched Mike prac-
> tice the violin. She looked up at Jim, her clear gray eyes
> shining, and motioned him not to interrupt. Jim clapped
> his big hands over his ears and walked out.
> He was part way to the corral when he stopped and

stared, for his older son was riding the milk cow. "Joey!" Jim cried, running toward the fence. "Get off that cow! You want sour milk for supper?"

"Okay, Pa," the boy said and slid off the cow's back. He was short and stockily built, with a fine fuzz showing on his cheeks.

"If you've a mind for exercise you can begin shovelin' out this corral!" Jim leaned against the fence, breathing heavily. Then he looked at his son and added, "Didn't mean to yell at you, Joey. It's just—."

"That's okay," Joey said. "Listen, Pa, can I have a rodeo out here Sunday and invite the class?"

"No!" Jim shouted. "Think I spent my life learnin' to raise good steers so a bunch of kids can ride 'em thin?"

Joey frowned. "But I already asked the kids, Pa," he said.

"Then tell 'em I won't have it!" Jim said, and turned back to the house.

This is another scene of conflict that reveals the character of the son and the increasing emotional disturbance in the rancher. Note that here, in characterization, there is a repetition of the gentleness revealed in the opening scene with the porcupine; this is indicated when the rancher says he didn't mean to yell at Joey. Then the rancher loses his temper and responds violently to his son's rodeo suggestion, indicating the rancher's emotional upheaval as a result of his daughter's leaving.

Inside, the violin was still being worked over by his younger son, but Mary was in the kitchen starting supper. She paused beside him and put her hand on his shoulder. "Jim—," she began, and then stopped. The question in her mind showed in her eyes.

"Sue-Ellen's leavin'," he said. "She'll be finished packin' and gone by now."

Mary's mouth quivered and he wanted to hold her in his arms and feel her softness against him. In the living room the sounds from the violin had stopped. Mary turned and shouted, "Mike, get on with that practicing."

Mike appeared in the kitchen doorway, fair-skinned and blond-headed as Jim had been as a boy. "This stinky deal!" he said, glaring at the violin.

"Music lessons cost money," Mary said. "You practice."

Mike looked over at his father. "Is Sue-Ellen pullin' out, Pa?"

"Yes," Jim said shortly. "You better go check the sheep before supper."

"I can't, Pa. I gotta get started on a theme for Miss Murphy. I gotta have it in the mornin'. Ain't that a deal?"

"Isn't," Mary corrected. "Your grammar, Mike." She paused and said, "Play the waltz for me, honey. I always wanted to be a violinist." Her eyes became soft and dreamy. "There's nothing like music."

"Lord," Jim said when the boy had left, "you call *that* music?"

"Hush, Jim!" Mary cried. "Let me think of something besides Sue-Ellen."

"I can't," he said dully. He picked up his hat. "I better check the sheep."

This third scene rounds out the family situation, reveals Mary's character, and again indicates the pressure of the problem that is the center of the story. Repetition has been used to drive home to the reader the significance of the problem in relation to the characters. Also, it is well to consider here how much the addition of the two boys means to the story. They bring variation and depth and color to the author's original concept of characterization, which was to have only

three people in the story. They provide a means of revealing Mary's character through her attitude toward
music and her attempts to keep from dwelling on the
leaving of her daughter. The father's reaction to them
gives the author a chance to do more characterization
with him, to draw more attention to the conflict within
him, and to move the plot forward, covering ground toward some sort of solution. Apart from this, the boys
contribute a lifelike atmosphere of family relations that
could not have been achieved had only Mary and Jim
been carrying the story at this time. Some background
color has also been added through the boys.

The rewards of the unexpected

Again, it is important to remember that in the process of developing the story, in the beginning only the
bare bones of the plot were in evidence. The boys furnished some of the covering for those bones. It is my
conviction that had the boys not come unexpectedly
into the story in the writing of it, the middle part of
the story (following the first scene of clash between father and daughter) would have fallen apart, and I
would have been in trouble. The writer must learn to
trust—particularly in his first draft—the unexpected
elements that creep in as he works freely and quickly
with his imagination. This is one of the most fascinating and rewarding aspects of writing; it is what happens because of that element of looseness in the plot.
The writer must realize that all he plots through his
character or characters before he begins writing is only
a *guide* or *indication* of what the fully developed story
may be. And it is only when he knows with enthusiasm

and conviction the problem and personality of the main character that other characters may spring into being to complement the main one. This is simply the cumulative effect of directed creative activity, and such activity can only happen when the writer knows what he has to work with.

> He knew Sue-Ellen and Roy were gone when he got to the lower ranch. The curtainless windows reflected the red fire of sunset. He drove past, making a mental note to stop and milk the cows on his way back.
>
> As he went up the long slope toward the fenced pasture, he saw the sheep there above him—three hundred purebreds with black faces, drifting slowly toward the flatter land with the blazing sunset behind them. He recalled suddenly the words of an old sheepman he had worked for as a boy: "Sheep don't like to look into the sunset, lad. It's too bright for their eyes. They'll go east with the evening."

The reader will see that here—at last—I have worked in the poetic line that stimulated me to think in story terms. At this point in the writing of the story, I had no idea as to how I would use this line; I only knew I must somehow work it into the conclusion. But, when I had *finished writing* that paragraph, I knew at once how the line would be used. As soon as I knew this, I had to make the main character aware of the significance of the line. The next paragraph is a result of this need.

> He stopped the truck and sat quietly, the words ringing as clear in his mind as the tinkle of the sheep's bells. Beyond the flock, in the higher pastures, he saw his cattle standing dark against the crimson sky line.

Mary had supper waiting when he got home. "It took you a long time," she said.

"Yes," Jim replied. It had taken him years, he thought, but he didn't tell Mary that. Nor was there any need to tell her now that Mike wouldn't ever be a musician or that Joey might never want to carry on the ranches.

When supper was over, he asked the boys to do the dishes. "Mary, we're goin' for a little ride," he said. "I've got something to tell you."

She put on the torn sweater she wore outdoors to feed the chickens, and they got into the truck and drove down the narrow dirt road. When they came to the lower ranch, Jim turned in. "Get out," he said. "Come inside." And he held her small, strong hand tightly as he led her into the kitchen. He turned on the electric lights.

"Mary," he said, and drew a deep breath, "we're movin' back here. I'll sell the other place or hire a man to run it. This is yours—always will be—if it suits you."

She touched the shining gas stove and the new sink. He saw a gleam of tears in her eyes. "It's fine, Jim," she said, "only—only I wish it could have been for Sue-Ellen. She's young. We're not, not any more."

For a moment a terrible ache was in Jim's throat and then he smiled. "We're still young, Mary," he said. "We just forgot it for a while."

He looked at Mary, and realized it was true. She was still young—and even the torn sweater couldn't take away any of the beauty that was there. He reached out and brushed her hair back gently. "The way I figure it, Mary," he said, "a man can't live his kids' lives. It's hard to learn that, but it's true. And there's something else I want you to think about: A strong man shouldn't be afraid to look into the sunset—by himself, without his kids to lean on."

Then he put his arms around her, holding her hard. "It's only sheep," he said, "that go east with the evening."

The main character has solved his problem; its solution was suggested by the poetic line about the sheep. The final scene is one in which husband and wife draw closer together, in which the rancher turns from trying to possess his daughter and from all future plans of possessing his sons and keeping the house for them. He has given his children freedom and at the same time has discovered he has a life of his own to live. The theme is evident. The story was published in short-short form with the title, "A Life of Our Own." No revisions were necessary except the small corrections of spelling and punctuation made in doing a clean copy from the rough draft.

In thinking over the development of this story from the three strands of interest taken from life and embellished to make fiction, the reader should be able to see that plot is no pattern dreamed up aside from people. He should see also how the plot of a story may develop in the course of the writing of it, moving beyond what the writer has conceived before he puts a word on paper. And if the beginning writer will simply say to himself, "People make the plot," he has taken a first and basic step forward in the understanding of a technique he must master.

CHAPTER 11

DIALOGUE WITH DISTINCTION

THERE'S an old saying, "Every time she opens her mouth, she puts her foot in it." The same situation is too often true of our fictional characters. They get us into difficulty because they say the wrong things, say nothing, or say too much. They don't contribute to the movement of the story and what we achieve on paper, through dialogue, becomes dull, chatty, or words existing in a void.

Dialogue must move a story. When people talk on the printed page, they must characterize themselves or others in the story, must reveal aspects of background or convey information necessary to the story, must expose motivations, point toward the theme, help create atmosphere or develop the plot. Dialogue is intimately related to the whole substance of a story.

Dialogue that does not relate to the author's conception of his story cannot be anything but chatty, dull, ineffectual. It can't go anywhere. This happens in the work of beginning writers over and over again. It happens because they aren't sure about what they have to say, about the kind of people who will say it, and because they haven't revised their dialogue to try to make it distinctive.

What can the writer do? He can first take more time to know the substance of what he wants to write and to know his characters. He can listen to friends and strangers and become thoroughly acquainted with the things they say that reveal their reactions to various situations. He can become aware of their speech rhythms, their speech tags—those repeated words or phrases that have become habitual. In such listening the writer will become aware too of the aimlessness of most talk. Fiction demands that it be anything but aimless, that it be culled, sharpened, varied, directed. And the writer can read, especially plays, to become aware of the potential of the spoken word. He can study a variety of magazines that print fiction, short story anthologies, and pay particular attention to dialogue. These efforts will help him to understand what is meant by directed and distinctive dialogue.

Stories that open with dialogue require more skill than the average beginning writer possesses. Dialogue that stands alone, particularly in the opening of a story, is seldom effective and is rarely found in the work of the most distinguished fiction writers of the past or present. Description, author comment, the establishing of setting and situation form the background for dialogue. We reveal in greater degree, confirm, drive home with dialogue what we have already hinted, indicated, suggested.

Insofar as the beginning writer is concerned, he must avoid dialogue that doesn't say anything and must remember that good dialogue doesn't start from scratch. The author must keep in mind that when his fictional characters meet and speak, his readers and these characters must have been prepared for that meeting. In other words, the opening of a short story should give the reader an understanding of the story characters before they open their mouths. This applies to the main character in particular. The writer must generally present him *in situation* before dialogue with the other characters in the story can be effective. When the main character and other characters in the story meet, they *do things to each other with words.* They please, intrigue, offend, challenge, according to the opening of the story. The beginning writer should keep in mind that to accomplish this successfully, he must know his characters inside and out and also must know before he starts, what his story is going to be about.

After the opening scene or scenes of a story, the beginning writer may find his story falling apart not because he doesn't know where he is going or because his characters aren't using directed conversation, but because the speech of his characters hangs in what I classify as a void. This isn't an example of chatty conversation that's too long, too repetitious, too pass-the-time-of-day sort of thing. The words are good words, strong words, words relating directly to the whole of the story, but they don't come through to the reader or to the listener, if the story is being read aloud. The mind wanders, the reader yawns. Again, as in the opening of the story, we need props. And props of a particular kind. We need a sense of movement, a sense of variation in the characters themselves or in their surroundings to make the dialogue more meaningful, to tie it down. We need a reminder of something happening other than the spoken word.

If two characters are talking inside a house, for instance, after a few bare lines of dialogue supported only by "he said," or "she said," the author may indicate through one of the characters a blowing curtain, the sound of a car, a pattern of sunlight on the floor, a scent of dust or food, flowers—anything to stimulate the senses of the reader and pull him back into the scene. Even the physical movement of one of the characters is often enough to take the dialogue out of a void. For example, "He walked a few steps and turned." Or, "He drew back the curtain." Or, "She plucked nervously at the threads in her scarf."

Passages of dialogue may be supported by objective or subjective thinking of the main character. Objective: "He considered her coldly, knowing now that nothing she could say would reach him." Subjectively: "I've lost all feeling for her. Nothing she says can get to me."

The dialogue may be interspersed with flashbacks— brief flashbacks in which the main character recalls similar scenes or contrasting scenes. These may be presented objectively or subjectively.

Author comment may be used to prevent long passages of dialogue from existing in a void. Between speeches of the characters the author may inject a few lines such as these: "In the distance, thunder rumbled, and a fierce gust of wind swept into the room bringing the scent of dust and coming rain." Or, "The corners of the room began to fill with darkness and soon only their faces stood out, pale and strange." A line such as this also indicates the passage of time and of conversation, and is followed by more conversation adding to the intensity of the scene.

It is not to be assumed from all this that there are never passages of conversation that may stand alone with a use, now and then, of the "he said" and "she said." One finds such paragraphs written with great skill in novels or short stories, but dialogue of this kind has been prepared for to the extent that the reader needs no props. He knows who is speaking, and how and why. Sometimes he may read several paragraphs and not need to be reminded who is talking. Dialogue of this kind can be used only when the reader (and the writer) knows the rising action of the plot, knows the characters very well, and has already predicted possible outcomes of the immediate scene. Few professional writers can approximate what Hemingway does in "The Killers," in which dialogue carries the entire story and is used with very few props.

Flavor and technique

Granted that we understand the necessity of dialogue that ties into the story and moves it, and dialogue that must be supported by props to keep the story from taking place in a void, what can we do to improve dialogue in our fiction?

The writer should always remember that "said" is the best verb he can use in most instances. The day of stories with unusual verbs, verbs the author strained to find, is past. The hero no longer "grits," "expostulates," or "snarls" when he's talking. In reading aloud, if you feel self-conscious about the repetition of "said," remember it will not affect the silent reader in the same way.

Contractions help to give dialogue vitality and a feeling of naturalness. "Can't" is better than "cannot." In listening to the talk of people around him, the writer can become aware of the use of contractions. He will also notice them in his reading.

Conveying technical information through dialogue needs watching. For that matter, conveying technical information any time in writing fiction needs careful handling. In dialogue, colorful aspects of factual information regarding any vocation may be presented in varying sentence lengths. The additional information is best covered quickly in author comment or in an offhand recording by one of the characters of his thinking or observation. Sometimes, after one highlight of a technical background for a story is presented, the rest may be dismissed simply by saying, "Jim talked on, explaining the whole business while they finished their lunch."

What is known in editorial offices as "the question technique" should be used sparingly in dialogue, and also in monologue, where the character is revealing his own thoughts in talking to himself. Too many questions weaken conversation and give the dialogue a lack of forward movement and positive implication. The same is true where we have a character talking inside himself. For example: "What's happened to us? Where did our marriage start falling apart? Why does love seem a series of polite gestures with no warmth?" Editors I have known would rather have such a passage handled in the following manner: "What had happened to their marriage? Love was a series of polite gestures with no warmth and everything between them was falling apart like a frail building with no foundations."

Flavor may be given to dialogue by having characters talk according to their education, their background, their occupation. A ranch hand would never say, "May I have a cigarette?" He would say, "Gimme a smoke," "Hand me the makin's," or "Got a cigarette?" College professors do not always talk in the manner that they use in the classroom. At home, in anger, or in love, they may resort to incomplete sentences, dangling participles, odd little tags of speech that are related to their childhood.

All speech is changed according to circumstances. In scenes of fast action, dialogue (like action) is couched in short sentences. Strong emotions always contribute to broken sentences, incomplete utterances, words that suggest rather than tell all that is happening. The writer trying to write his first love scene will soon discover that it's easy to talk love to death. Love scenes, like death scenes, are most effective with limited dialogue and plenty of props.

The inner speech of a character should match his dialogue. If, in speaking to his girl, a truck driver says "ain't," it wouldn't be his way of talking to himself to say, "Honey, I'm not coming home the long road tonight." If the author is talking about *his* thoughts and feelings, that's another thing. The author will, of course, use correct, as well as colorful, language. When a character speaks in a manner quite different from that of his companions or in a way that seems foreign to his job, the author must supply reason for this.

Dialect

The flavor of dialogue is often brought about through the use of dialect. Few writers can write thick or heavy dialect and expect anyone to read what they've written. It's better to *suggest* dialect by using a few key words and phrases rather than faithfully reproduce dialect as it is often heard. For instance, take a line of Scottish dialect. In true dialect the line, "I can't go away," would be written, "I canna gang awa'." This is too much even for the reader most sympathetic toward dialect. The flavor of dialect is created by saying, "I canna go away."

This same method of suggesting should be used in writing dialogue where characters habitually drop the "g" in words ending in "ing." If the writer drops a "g" in the beginning of a speech, he need not continue to do so; a cow puncher may be "workin' " cattle in one line and "going" to town in the next. The flavor is there.

To return to the use of dialect, no writer should use it unless he is familiar enough with it to think in it without trouble. When I wrote my first novel, *Fire in the Water,* I had spent thirty nights at sea with herring fishermen and was familiar enough with their dialect, at the thickest, to be able to speak it or write it or think it with ease. In writing the book, I cut it down to a minimum, but the total effect was the same as that given by the use of complete dialect.

Beware of flowery, over-poetic dialogue. People don't talk that way to each other. On the printed page such dialogue becomes obviously ornate, stuffy, and unreal. Your characters may, in deep emotion, think poetically, and the author commenting may write brief poetic passages, but this can't go into the words two people use to each other.

Reading a story aloud or having someone else read your story aloud will help you become aware of dialogue. When I first started to write I had much trouble with dialogue. The moment my people started to talk, the story became burdened, unreal. By reading my own work aloud, I discovered that no people I could imagine on earth or in heaven would talk as my characters talked.

The beginner should remember that the writing of dialogue is, like all other aspects of creating fiction, an exploratory experience. It is only as the writer knows his people, his story substance, that he experiments to relate the dialogue to these in a satisfactory pattern. Working and reworking, we discover what our characters should say, how they can say it most effectively, and how much should be implied rather than stated. *Good* dialogue does things *to* and *with* characters and *to* and *for* the reader.

CHAPTER 12

𝕏 THE ENCHANTMENT OF DESCRIPTION

ANYONE who writes understands what it is to fall under the spell of description. It is much like falling in love, for an intense affair with words develops. It is the most satisfying and natural kind of creative expression for the beginning writer. It is also the most dangerous, for used incorrectly it may clog the movement and meaning of the story. In the creation of fiction, description has impact only if it is woven into the whole of the story in the same way that bright threads might be woven into a piece of cloth. Good description makes fiction sparkle.

When I was twelve I wrote a description of the high cattle country of Colorado where I lived. It approached novella length and the teacher of our rural school was impressed to the point of awe—more by quantity than quality, I am sure. I was also impressed. This piece of writing had required no great effort on my part and what a flowing of sentences, what a glorious splashing of adjectives I had achieved!

Description in fiction

It wasn't until many years later that I made a startling discovery—my lengthy descriptions were what short story editors liked to cut out. I then realized that to get those landscape portraits past the editors I had to do three things—make them brief, make them memorable, and bind them inextricably to the movement of my story.

When I got ready to write my second novel, *So Far from Spring,* I knew the importance of blending characters, atmosphere, and background. This I had achieved in my first book, *Fire in the Water.* In *So Far from Spring,* I wished to describe that windy, mean, and beautiful cattle country where I grew up. But I did not present that description in one great lump as I had in grade school. Nor did it exist in a void where there were no people. It was intimately related to my characters and scattered through the building of my book—sometimes as cornerstones, sometimes as slender arches of transition, sometimes as windows or doors allowing the reader to peer into or enter the hearts and minds of the people. My description became a support for the completed structure of the novel. And description must do the same for a successful short story.

The word "support" implies several things—creating atmosphere, creating emotional impact, bridging time, illuminating character, painting the scenery, portraying action. When we take these together, we see that they help to establish that feeling of reality, of life.

How shall the beginning writer approach an understanding of the use of description in fiction? If he will
learn first to *observe accurately*, it will help. And once
having observed, he must be equally accurate in putting
his observations into words. Then, if he will link observation and expression tightly to his characters, he
will have eliminated much difficulty. I often tell my
students, "A window, a mountain, a tree is of no importance except as seen by men or women in the varied
climate of their emotions."

Let's consider, for a moment, the business of accurate observation, because this is so basic to creation.
Learn to look carefully, not carelessly. This necessi-
tates having the senses alert and the mind uncluttered.
We must be able to forget ourselves and really concentrate on the world around us. You will observe that this
doesn't often happen with people. Think how many
times you are in the company of those who have wan-
dering minds while they pretend to listen to what is
being said. Actually, they are so busy considering what
they wish to say that they can't possibly hear anything.
Writers are usually good listeners. And haven't you
walked on a mountain or by the sea with someone who
was oblivious to scene, who might as well have been
wearing blinders of some sort?

Observation, discrimination, imagination

The writer must move in the world of nature and
of people with an outgoing sense of expectancy. What
he learns depends on how much he can give of himself
to the observation of person, place, and thing, and this

act of giving, of allowing himself to be open to all sensory impressions, is implicit in the art of forgetting the self.

When it comes to a classification of what we observe, we move into the world of discrimination and imagination. Work to be specific. If you are going to describe trees, distinguish them as much as you would distinguish people. Pick out that particular angle or aspect you wish to stress. What is it you wish to convey about trees? Is it the sound when a gust of wind strikes the leaves? Is it the play of light or shadow on green motion? Or would you prefer making a particular tree come alive on paper by talking only of the fascinating space designs between the branches—especially noticeable in winter with those trees that shed their leaves? You will note that a tree does not look the same at high noon as in afternoon or evening or early morning. And it will have many variations in winter, spring, summer, and fall. Distance makes evergreens look black, not green.

Thinking in terms of description, consider snow. Snow takes on all sorts of colors other than white—silver by moonlight, pink in sunrise or sunset, lavender from shadows, green from the green light in certain evening skies. All objects cast their reflected color over it. Animals mark it with various designs. Wind picks it up and puts it down, altering, reworking, sculpturing. And look what snow does to things—to hills, streets, willows, roofs, rivers, window sills, dogs, children.

The writer can fill notebooks with observations of the world around him, observations of people and places, of moods and movements, of meanings and memories. And out of these materials he will take what he needs for description in his particular story or book. He will learn soon that sentences have to vary according to what he wishes to say. Action scenes, for instance, require short strong sentences with emphasis on verbs rather than adjectives. I quote a brief scene that's part of a description of herring fishing, from my first novel, *Fire in the Water:*

> Heavy sea boots thudded against the deck. Oaths ripped the air. Chains rattled. Ropes uncoiled like brown snakes. Men began casting the net from the stern, throwing overboard first the green buoy.

And here, from the same novel, a more intimate and more leisurely description of the sea at night:

> Rab listened to the slow wash of water off the bow. The night air was clean and sharp, with the breath of frost in it. The mainland, lying off to their left, had a luminous quality and the hills seemed buoyant, as though they floated in the mist of moonlight. The long, low-rolling swells were silvered on the crests, the troughs dark but changing with the shifting of the water—the darkness turning to light with the upward push of the waves, becoming silver and then shading off again into the dark.
>
> Aye, Rab thought, the moods of the sea—the stillness of it on an early morning with no wind blowing, the water pale gray, and the air as damp and soft as a mist against the cheek; the bleakness of it in winter when sleet pecks at the wheelhouse windows like the beaks of a thousand daft birds; the violence of it in a big blow with the waves coming at a boat like mountains and the boat seeming but a frail thing.

Both descriptions are based on first-hand, accurate observation, used with imagination and discrimination to suit each particular scene and situation. Choice of words and sentence structure are varied to fit the pace of the scenes. The reader will note the use of L-sound words in the first part of the second description.

In describing people it is much more important to know what is inside a character than what is on the outside; physical description is always secondary to what a character thinks and feels. Even in the novel, where the writer has more room for detail and may move at a slower pace, editors become impatient with too much physical description and not enough about the emotions of the characters. An editor once wrote on the margin of a page of mine: "I don't give a damn about this woman's clothes. What does she *feel?*"

I have written and sold short stories in which there was very little physical description of character and what there was didn't come along until the middle of the stories. I have also written stories that had emphasis on physical description in the opening paragraphs. Here is an example of such a paragraph, from my first slick story sale, "Osage Girl":

When I remember my Uncle Jed, I always see him the way he looked that day in Springfield, sitting easy on the sulky behind Osage Girl as she paced a half length ahead of the field of nine. That was the greatest race I ever saw Uncle Jed drive.

My Uncle Jed was a big man. He was over six feet tall and he weighed two hundred and ten pounds, but he walked lightly. There was nothing clumsy about Uncle Jed. He had a round red face and hair that was white even when he was young. His eyes were blue, and when he looked at horses they softened the way some men's eyes do when they look at a beautiful woman.

And here are some descriptive lines from the opening page of another short story:

> When he came to teach in the small junior college, he arrived in an old car with a lean dog riding beside him on the front seat. They got out and stood together in the amber sunlight of September. And it was as though the feel of impending autumn touched man and dog; it was as though the nostalgic air and the haze on the near mountain said, "They've come a long way and they've been looking for something a long time."
>
> Dan Montgomery was thirty but he had the kind of face that said he could be forty and that he would probably look the same at sixty. The lines around his mouth and eyes were not bitter; they only said that life had gotten to him.
>
> He was completely unaware that he wore dusty levis, a travel-stained shirt and that his hair hadn't been combed for some time. His clothes clung to him as though he shaped them to himself and extended beyond them . . .

One is most impressed by the power and enchantment of description in scenes of high emotion, such as those dealing with death or love. Here, the few lines of dialogue (too much can kill the meaning of either love or sorrow) are colored, given emotional impact by the descriptive words. These lines of description are taken from a scene in which a father says goodbye to a much-loved daughter:

> The sky and earth ran together as though in a great wash of rain. But he lifted his hand in a gay salute as the stage moved away and the dust rose behind it, and the face of his daughter was gone.
>
> Kelsey turned slowly back to his car. A dog stirred and yawned in front of the drugstore. Somewhere up the street a door slammed. He got in the car and sat for a

moment, trying to ease the sense of loss that filled him. The years of his living rushed over him in memories bitter and bright, and it seemed to him that all his days had been a hard journey toward some distant green where all things were good. He brought his big hand up and drew it across his eyes.

And from the same novel, *So Far from Spring*, here is a brief description, indicating the unhappy feeling of a man:

When he rode down the mountain everything changed, and it was only the same high country he had always known, the trees dark-massed and the night clogged with pine smell. An owl hooted. And the wind stirred, rising up from the floor of the Park like something that had slept and wakened unsatisfied from its sleeping. It moved the branches of the pines, rubbing them together with a sound that was like hurting.

From my novel, *The Oil Patch*, this is another example of description supporting emotion and helping to create additional emotional impact. The heroine has decided to end her marriage, and the scene follows the parting with her husband:

She walked heavily from the bedroom and into the kitchen where the door stood open, inviting her out and away from this last painful act of marriage. She stepped into the afternoon with its warm deceit. Did anyone doubt winter was coming? The wind moved against her, touching her gently, uncertain of its strength. Along the alley the brilliant fall weeds trembled in what might well be the last day of full color before the snows.

She walked until she came to the end of the row, going past the garbage cans, remembering the way rain sounded on their galvanized tin lids. She started across the prairie, hurrying now. Making haste toward what? She slipped and fell and felt the smarting cut on her leg. No matter. Let it bleed. She came to the top of a ridge and paused, confronted with the distance that discharged upon the wind the haunting promises of fulfillment.

Using the tools of poets

The writer will learn with practice where he can best use repetition, suggestion, brief or long poetic phrases in his descriptions. A few words of warning should be given here about the use of intense, poetic descriptions. They do not go well where the writer is describing a scene objectively. But they may be used with satisfying effect when put in the mind of the character. Here the author allows such poetical expression to spring from deep inside the character and to be free in form.

The fiction writer can improve his descriptive passages by becoming acquainted with all the technical tools of the poets, such as simile, metaphor, assonance, and alliteration. If he studies the devices of poetry, he will one day find himself thinking in words that fit certain aspects of landscape—rolling shapes and sounds of words to suit vast and rolling country and vice versa. He will learn to be careful with adjectives and use them sparingly. He will discover by reading his work aloud that certain rhythms of words fit exactly what he wishes to say while others do not.

The beginning writer can improve his descriptive powers by careful reading. He will see, for instance, that Pasternak in *Doctor Zhivago* uses color, particularly lavender, to create emotional undertones. He will try to understand how Conrad creates the atmosphere in the movement, the sound, the scent of the sea in his

descriptive phrases and how these curl around characters and events in such a way as to blend men and ocean
into one great interlocking pattern. He will look for
what James Joyce does with description in the stream-
of-consciousness type of writing or what Eudora Welty
accomplishes through descriptive words in presenting
the world of the jazz musician in her short story,
"Powerhouse." And when he reads in any book or
magazine a line that particularly appeals to him, he
should stop and reread it and ask himself how the
author accomplished this. What descriptive words
stand out? Where was the emphasis—on verb or adjec-
tive?

If he feels himself stale in description, it will help
to read poetry. The most accurate and unforgettable
description I have ever read of a trout is in a poem by
Gerard Manley Hopkins: ". . . rose moles all in stip-
ple upon trout that swim . . ."

Those who feel their descriptive writing has become
ineffectual may sometimes be helped by turning away
from outside observation entirely for a while and allowing imagination to play with mental concepts. For
instance, to think on any color for a length of time has
a tendency to provoke the imagination. I often ask my
class members to write freely everything or anything
that comes to them about the color blue or red or green
or purple.

Once for my own stimulation I recorded all the
sounds I thought rain would make falling in the alley
—rain falling on old window shades, on toadstools, on
tin cans, on wood, on faded newspapers. I didn't do
this while listening to rain but while listening to a

piece of modern experimental music that was distinguished by polytonality. The exercise stimulated me, grew into an interesting poem, and furnished all sorts of descriptive lines that might be used in a story with a rainy background.

Try, for example, recalling a series of odors—scents along riverbanks in early morning, in summer meadows, on the hills after rain, in certain clothing stores, on a downtown street at theater time, in leather shops, bakery shops, candy stores, at a carnival, on your own block. And this reminds me of T. S. Eliot's descriptive sentence in his poem, "Preludes,"—"The winter evening settles down/With smell of steaks in passageways." A strong descriptive line in poetry, and it would be equally strong used in prose.

Good description, like any other aspect of fiction writing, is rooted in awareness. And awareness, I think, is a part of love. It is an outgoing alliance with life, a desire to embrace it, to celebrate it. A feeling for place is as important as a feeling for people in the writing of description. I freely admit I have been carrying on a love affair with the state of Wyoming for many years. And while I have written of other places and of situations foreign to this particular region, it is my greatest pleasure to speak of the land I know better than any other and of the people who inhabit it and are influenced by it. I agree with Van Wyck Brooks who once said that the regional writer should feel strongly about the place where he lives and put as much of that place as possible into his writing. A better book or short story will result.

In awareness, we observe closely. In the sense of artistic creation, we know that to observe is not enough; we understand that we must touch this with imagination and narrow it with selectivity. We must, to describe creatively, be as much concerned with what we leave out as with what we put in. We look at meadows or hills much as we look at the face of a friend, seeing many things, seeing contradictions, confusions, dominant lights and shadows. We wish to make earth or person a meaningful whole. Art does not deal in confusions. Art, like love, works at putting things in their proper places, under the correct light, for the desired emphasis.

CHAPTER 13

ℵ Writers, Speak Now!

Some time ago, Robert Tristram Coffin wrote in a poem, "There is strange holiness around/ Our common days on common ground . . ." What he meant, of course, is that the business of ordinary day-to-day living need not be a drab and uninspiring experience. It's all in the way you see it.

Time is still with us, and the earth—we hope—shall remain the home (or at least one of the homes) of man. But what has happened to that "strange holiness"— that exhilarating sense of inspiration, of challenge, of fulfillment?

We hear that television is desperately in need of "fresh material," that magazine editors are looking for "distinctive fiction," that book publishers search for "moving stories that intrude on mind and emotions," that movie producers are desperate for a story "with real meat in it."

All this indicates that something is happening in our country, and more specifically, something is happening to writers. While it is true that editors have always sought the kind of material mentioned, today's cry is louder and more persistent than ever before. And who shall answer, if not the writers?

But we should look first at the reasons for this lack of superior material, and it is apparent there *is* a lack, despite the fact that many writers insist editors will not recognize good material and that professional authors are receiving rejection slips as never before.

In today's fast-paced world with its many confusions, the mind may be likened to a food chopper into which everything is tossed. What comes out, in most instances, can scarcely be classified as meaningful. Living has become a sort of grab bag in which the more one gets hold of, the more one is supposed to know. The more books one can read—skimming like a bird from page to page —the more knowledge one shall possess. The more activities one participates in, the more one reaches out to squander self, the more enriched are one's days on this earth. In this obsessive pursuit of emotional, mental, and physical surfeiting, man is not so much exploring life as escaping from the meaning of existence.

The root of creativity

A writer dare not become a part of this all too prevalent pattern. When he reads, he must have time to savor the richness of another writer's words, and he must be able to take their meaning and make it a part of his own life. He must not become a victim of mental cramming in which a hodgepodge of facts, opinions, images are taken in one huge gulp. A mind filled with such material cannot view a neighbor, a sky, or an earth with any sharp sense of awareness—and to be aware is vital to a writer's existence, for it is the root of his creativity. And creativity is, in turn, the root of his survival, and may ultimately mean the survival of all men.

With the constant emphasis on speed, many people become so conscious of the atmosphere of haste that they cannot concentrate on any one thing for a given length of time. The writer dare not allow himself to be afflicted with this jumpy mental state. Writing, as no other work, requires complete concentration. A writer's relation to an idea or the act of writing that idea must be a whole giving of himself. Few people today give themselves fully in any activity. Their attention is diversified. The experience at hand is seldom tasted fully and completely, for the mind is already jumping ahead to another experience.

With the publishing challenges facing him today, the writer should first ask himself if he is willing to give the time and concentration to his work that will be required—if he is to write superior material, and write it he must if he expects to sell. He should ask himself, particularly if he is a beginner, if he is going deliberately to plan to read fully and carefully the work of some of the best authors who have published, yesterday and today. He should ask himself if he is strong enough to turn a deaf ear to the continuous outside demands on his time and energy. He should ask himself if what he has written has been approached in the right way, if he has given himself the necessary quiet hours to explore the basic materials of his art and craft. This means the turning over of an idea for days or weeks or months, if necessary. It also means taking an *empty* mind with him on a walk or a ride and seeing, really seeing, his friends, his neighbors, himself. It means noting the exact color of a cloud or the texture of a tree trunk or the fascinating space patterns between the branches.

If he is "skimming" through his observations of people and earth and sky, as some people skim the pages of a book, he is not becoming a writer, no matter how long he has written or how much he has sold. He is living on the surface and he will find it increasingly difficult to turn out material that might find a home in today's markets.

Should the financial pressures of maintaining home and family be so great he feels he cannot take time to observe closely, to read more comprehensively, to write his best, then he should have a simple job that will enable him to provide basic necessities, and though he write less, it should be of high quality.

Human nature in crisis

In view of the difficulty of selling to today's markets, the writer should ask himself with all honesty if he is only attempting a carbon copy of what he has already seen on the television screen, on the magazine pages, or between the covers of a book. He cannot hope to succeed by emulating Hemingway or Camus or Frank O'Connor or any of the excellent or competent writers in today's popular magazines. His material must be his own—fresh, honest, vibrant—out of the multicolored world of his experience.

He should remind himself that the buyer of words—whether that buyer be in New York, Hollywood, or the

home town—wants something for his money. He does
not want a "skim" job or a job copied in the style of
someone else, nor does he want a "gimmick" treatment.
Many writers, especially beginners, get stuck on the
assumption that all they need is a gimmick.

The viewing public is sick unto death of "gimmicks"
and so are the directors and producers of television.
People do not experience any sense of a heightened
awareness of life or living from gimmicks. *They experience it from the revelation of human nature in crisis.*
Magazine editors do not want a story that has only a
"cute gimmick" to offer; they want a story that says
something warm and real about people—whether the
story be presented in a very light or a very serious manner. And the hometown editor doesn't want a feature
story or an article or a book review that is full of *forced*
cleverness rather than a freshness that has grown inevitably out of the writer's honest conception of his
material.

The writer should remind himself that there is not
and has never been any substitute for emotion. For
some reason, perhaps a pseudo-sophistication in a literary sense, there are writers who have deliberately
tried to handle words in a way that eliminates any emotional connotation. This is *cold* writing which is as bad
as sloppy writing inundated with sentimentality. But I
would rather read a writer who got sentimental here
and there than one who gave me the impression I might
be reading statistical information. Many of the fine
writers become sentimental at times. It has been a
criticism aimed at John Steinbeck, for instance. But in

Steinbeck there is also depth and beauty and majesty of characterization. The cold writers turn nothing loose—neither passion nor pain, beauty nor truth.

Poetry has been written by those who make it a sort of mental gymnastics, playing with words as they might play with lifting weights or tossing balls—objects with no relation to human emotions. The outstanding poets of our time have not done this. Who can read Dylan Thomas' poem on his thirtieth birthday without feeling the color and movement and all the emotional impact connected with that particular day in his life? It is a poem that will be read long after the work of the word jugglers has been forgotten.

Let the writer remember that in today's hectic world people are often numb to any sincere emotion. They recognize the need for it and the lack of it, but often they feel helpless to do anything about it. They observe that in much of our society it has become a *faux pas* to reveal emotion about anything. If, in many instances, a meaningful conversational topic is approached, many draw back for fear of ridicule of any expression of individual emotion and opinion. This does not make for enriched or happy living—it only makes for more loneliness and an increasing sense of futility in human communication.

But people desire to experience meaningful emotion and to understand themselves as well as others. They are hungry for stories in magazines or on the screen that allow them to share the vagaries of the heart, the courage of the human spirit, the vision of the dedicated mind. And if the writer, beginning or professional, understands what he is—a communicator of insights and ideas—then he must know that he cannot turn from the recognition of his emotions and the translation of these into the ordered emphasis of his art.

Makers of meanings

How can we possibly present meaning in human relationships unless our readers *care* what happens to the characters in our stories? And they cannot care unless the writer cares and allows himself to write with feeling. And to write with feeling, he must live with feeling, being able to give himself completely to experience. This, as I have pointed out, demands discrimination in the use of time. It means the deliberate search into the self and the deliberate and necessary standing aside, at times, from all the confusion, the noise, the chaos of propaganda, opinion, criticism. *For the writer must be of the world and yet out of it, and it is the balancing of this dual existence that becomes imperative if he is to preserve himself as a person and his talent as a tool of communication.*

One has only to be part of an audience to know with how much indifference people view what they see. Who cares what happens to the hero or heroine if the story is a rehash, a tired job? A drama—?—may be taking place, but it is often a drama of dead words, not flesh and blood. Yes, it consumes time while people, hungry for more than food, keep on eating popcorn and candy, yawning, thinking of something else, even trying to read or sew or work a crossword puzzle. The viewer gives only a little corner of himself to the picture before him. This is worse than half a loaf: It is a dusty crumb.

One may blame the publishers, the advertisers, the world situation; one may blame the producers, Hollywood, the actors. But in realistic analysis, the writer can blame only himself. The publisher does not deliberately publish a story that says nothing; the Hollywood director does not happily offer poor drama. Most publishers, producers, directors—as well as writers—are respectful of honest talent. But honest talent, real talent, doesn't try to pass off a thin story, a poor characterization, a "gimmick package."

The importance of individuality

Today, as never before, it is important that the writer stay at his desk and write, not only because the markets for the printed word are fewer and tougher to make; not only because of the great need in the field of television; but also for a reason that is even more important than these: *The writer must express himself because he is an individual in a world where individuality is fast disappearing.*

Perhaps I am old-fashioned, but I am glad I went to school when my teachers read what I wrote and took enough interest in me as a person to point out, in the worst of my work, a fine phrase here and a fresh thought there—even if my spelling wasn't always correct. It was close and personal communication. I felt like an individual, not a name grouped under "retarded," "advanced," "average," or "superior."

It need not be pointed out what will happen in a world in which people no longer exist as unique and special in themselves.

Why do I choose to say this to writers? Because we are first, last, and always *creators*. We are makers of meanings. If a stone wall must come down or a cloud be rent, we must do it with words. I am often told that too many people are writing or trying to write. My answer is, "Let there be more!" I can only add, as I did recently to a class of mine, "Speak out, speak up! Express what you are and what is yours. Say it the best way you can—not for money or for publication, although it is to be hoped some of you will enjoy the privilege of selling and sharing on the printed page. But speak *first* for the glory of expressing yourself, for the influence of the individual may function everywhere—in his home, his town, his community, his world. And it is on this alone that the future of our universe may one day depend."

The writers must function to full capacity. It is the obligation of all writers—professional, amateur, novice—to dedicate themselves as never before to creation —for the joy of the productive life, for the hope of more understanding, for the dream of communication —communication basic and warm and real, from man to man in a universe where each of us must search endlessly for the meaning of himself.

This is the world of that "strange holiness" the poet meant. It is the world in which man must never be so confused or so harassed that he cannot think his own thoughts and develop them into expression. It is the world in which no one should be ashamed of emotion, but glad that he is capable of feeling it. It is the world in which one should count it a privilege to walk the earth and look at the stars and move with the rhythms of seasons and tides. It is the world in which the writer should know himself as a giant among men—for in him, in what he experiences, is the root of creation. His obligation to himself and to all men is to put down firmly and honestly and beautifully what he knows.